THE CEARCHALL
TRACING THE LOST LIFE OF MARY GAUGHAN FROM ACHILL ISLAND TO GLASGOW

KEVIN GORMAN

For the people of Achill Island—past, present, and still to come.

Copyright © 2025 by Kevin Gorman

All rights reserved.

No part of this book may be reproduced in any form or by any electronic or mechanical means, including information storage and retrieval systems, without written permission from the author, except for the use of brief quotations in a book review.

❀ Formatted with Vellum

"Goodbye to Achill, I hate to leave you, It's a beautiful place for strangers; There's food and drink there and a thousand welcomes, for Achill is my home."

A verse added by the people of Achill to the 'A Farewell Song" by Br. Paul Carney (1895).

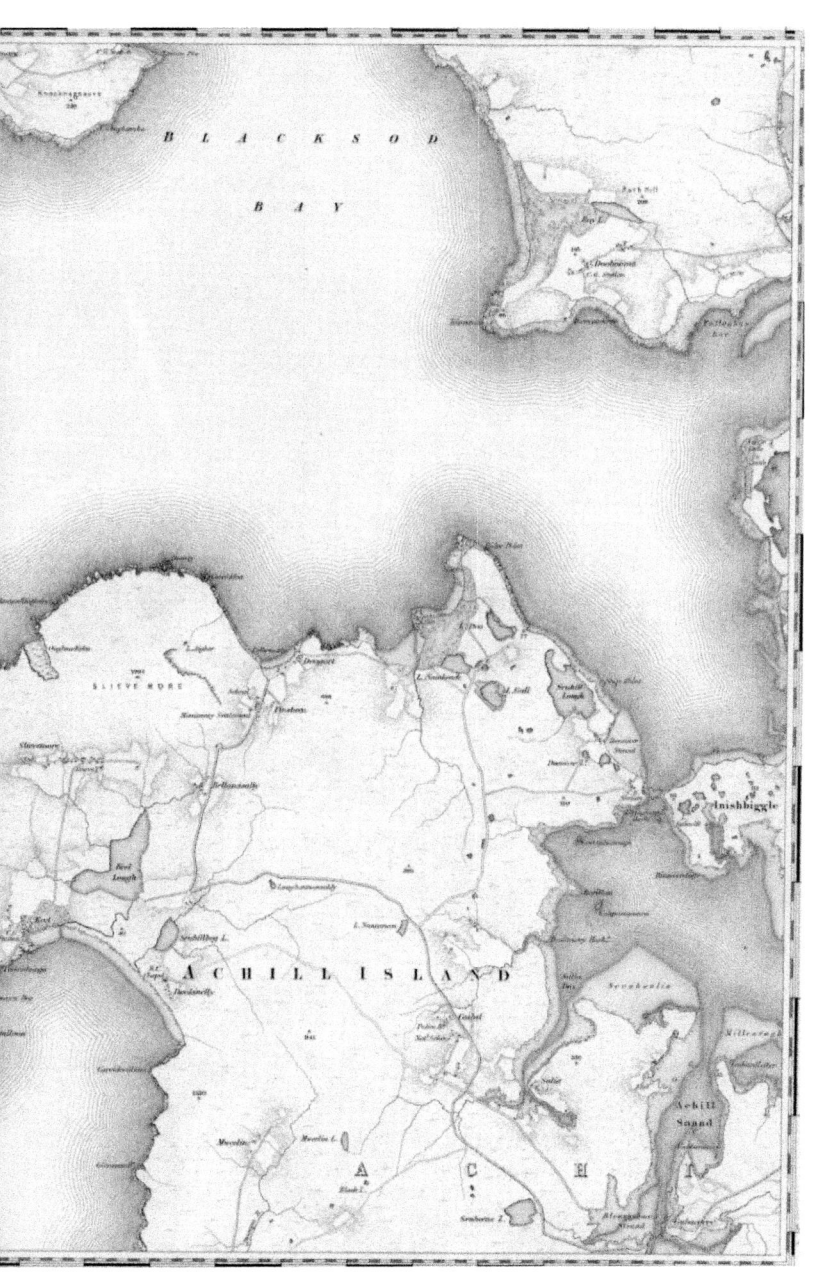

AUTHORS NOTE

I always knew we had Irish roots. Our surname made that clear, and so did a faint, half-remembered name—*Gaughan*—that I once overheard my late uncle, James Gorman, mention when I was about fourteen. But more than that, it was the places where the Gormans had made their homes in Glasgow: neighbourhoods woven with Catholic churches, Irish halls, and the green devotion of Celtic Football Club. Tradition was everywhere, in the air we breathed. Yet for years it remained only a surface understanding—until I began to look deeper.

Research came naturally to me, honed by a degree in History, and I had the persistence for it. But Irish genealogy is no gentle pastime. Records are incomplete, and names twist and wander—Gormal became Gorman, Gaughan turned into Geoghan or Goughan. First names echo through generations like family refrains: Henry and Harry, Catherine and Kate, and always, Mary. In time, everything begins to blur. Still, I kept chipping away.

Over the years, I pieced fragments together. Sometimes I would leave it for months; other times I returned like a detective revisiting a cold case. Eventually, I traced the Gormans back five generations. But one figure remained elusive: my great-grandmother, Mary Gaughan.

Her Irish origin was not a secret. My grandfather's army records listed her birthplace as the Irish Free State, and her children's names appeared clearly in Glasgow's Royston and Springburn districts—the Garngad of old. But two vital documents were missing: her marriage certificate and any death record in Glasgow. Their absence gnawed at me.

At the Mitchell Library's genealogy centre, I turned to the Glasgow Poor Law records from 1900 to 1930. I hadn't booked ahead, but when I explained I'd travelled up from England, a kind librarian bent the rules. She showed me the database, found me a desk, and let me dig. What I uncovered there changed everything.

Those ledgers opened a door to a place I had never heard of: Achill Island, County Mayo. I didn't even know it was an island. Yet its people had been part of my world for as long as I had been alive.

I never set out to write a book. There are no famous names in my family tree, no notorious branches—only ordinary Irish-Scots families working and enduring in industrial Scotland. Yet what unfolded was more than genealogy; it became a story of survival, identity, and quiet strength.

Mary began as little more than a mystery—a name scrawled on a certificate, a faint line in a census return. What compelled me was not my own family connection, but her story itself: the wildness of Achill, the tide of migration that carried its children to Scotland, the back-breaking labour of the tattie fields, and the quiet endurance that marked her life. What began as a search for context became an act of recovery. Piece by piece, her life emerged—not through family stories, but through what was left behind:

poor relief applications in Glasgow and Paisley, a child's death in Clydeside, a tenancy in the Garngad, and a mystery around her death.

Others helped me fill the gaps. The staff at the Mitchell Library in Glasgow guided me through the records. Bryan Smith at the Paisley Heritage Centre unearthed fragments from Renfrewshire. Brendan Walsh at the North Mayo Heritage Centre anchored the family to Achill's soil.

Researching a woman like Mary is never easy. Working-class, Irish, and poor—these are the lives least recorded, least preserved. Genealogy becomes more than a list of dates; it becomes an effort to give voice to someone history forgot.

Mary's life was not marked by fame, but by resilience. She lived through famine echoes, emigration, poverty, war, and the loss of children. Yet she raised a family that endured. Her legacy is not found on plaques or in books—until now. It lives in bloodlines, in memory, and in the resting place she returned to beneath the wind-swept slopes of Slievemore.

In tracing her steps, I found more than a name.

I found a presence.

WHERE THE WIND BEGINS

F amily history usually begins with the basics: births, marriages, deaths. Certificates form a breadcrumb trail from one generation to the next. But with Mary Gaughan, the trail was broken. No marriage certificate named her parents.

So I turned to census records. The Scottish returns of the 1870s and 1880s gave me too many Gaughans, too many dead ends. Newspaper searches offered nothing. I was chasing shadows.

Then, in an unexpected place—a blog by another frustrated researcher—I found a clue. They mentioned Poor Law records.

Before state welfare, the destitute turned to parish relief. Not all records survived, but Glasgow's had. And there, in the fragile ledgers of 1903, Mary Gaughan's name appeared. In applying for relief, she had named her parents: Henry Gaughan and Mary O'Donnell.

That single line opened everything. With those names, I searched the Irish indexes. I never found Mary's own birth, but her siblings appeared, all with the same parents.

More importantly, the records pointed to a place: Achill Island, County Mayo, and a village called Dooagh.

When I told my father what I had discovered—that his grandmother was from Achill—his response was immediate. He'd suffered a serious stroke the year before, and his memory wasn't great, but something seemed to stir. "That's right," he said, as if a long-buried memory had flickered back to life. Then he added something unexpected: "I remember a photograph of a woman kneeling at a grave... on a hillside, or beneath a mountain."

At the time, I let the comment pass. But that image lingered—the outline of a woman bent in grief, a mountain rising behind her. It seemed almost like a vision, a fragment from another life. Later, when I found myself standing among the leaning stones of the Old Cemetery at Slievemore, that memory would return—not just as my father's recollection, but as something I too had seen with my own eyes.

For now, I had two places to begin: Paisley, where Mary had worked, and Achill, where she was born.

I chose Achill.

I
OILEÁN ACLA

Achill Island—Oileán Acla—has been described in many ways over the centuries. Some say its name comes from the eagles that once soared above its cliffs. Others, like historian Bernard O'Hara, suggest it simply means "lookout" or "prospect." Whatever its origin, the name feels true. Achill has always been a place on the edge—of Ireland, of Europe, of history itself.

Its people, too, have often been judged from outside. Visitors called them "forgotten," "primitive," even "incorrigible." Such words reflected prejudice more than truth. When I began tracing the story of Mary Gaughan, those old portrayals fell away. What I saw instead was poverty, yes, but also endurance—a quiet, stubborn survival that defined the community she came from.

In the nineteenth century, Achill remained a world apart. Irish was the language of home and hearth, and Gaelic customs shaped the rhythm of daily life. English had reached the schools, yet even in the 1870s visitors were struck by how easily children switched between the two tongues. In the old days, in parts of Lower Achill, people still greeted one another with "Ó a ghráidh", "Oh, my love." It was a custom that earned them the affectionate nickname *Graidhíní*.

During Mary's time, the mainland was still a mystery to some of the older residents; some had never seen a train or set foot in a town. Though Achill is the largest island off Ireland's coast, until 1887 it was connected to the rest of Mayo only on paper. Real connection came when the Michael Davitt Bridge joined Achill Sound to the mainland; until then the island stood apart.

That isolation did not shield it from tragedy. In January 1839, Achill was battered by one of the fiercest storms in Irish history—*Oíche na Gaoithe Móire*, the Night of the Big Wind. Boats were smashed, roofs torn away, crops flattened from Dooagh to Dugort. At the Protestant Mission in Dugort, the buildings were spared, which some saw as divine protection. Others whispered darker explanations, blaming restless spirits forced back into the hills.

Less than a decade later came famine. Between 1841 and 1851, Achill's population fell from 6,392 to 4,950. In Keel, soldiers escorted eviction squads through the village. Thatch roofs were pulled down and torched. Families were marched under guard to the Westport workhouse. "This was my father's house and his father's before him," one man is reported to have said, before turning away for the last time.

Even the sea offered no refuge. In November 1847, a sudden storm drowned nineteen Keel fishermen within sight of shore. Fourteen widows were left behind, with thirty-eight children now fatherless. The grief carried across the island like a tide.

Amid such loss, visitors noted what they witnessed. The American Quaker Asenath Nicholson, travelling through

Mayo in the 1840s, found not only hunger but humanity. Women, hollow-eyed with want, still offered her bread. Children asked not for food but whether she needed rest. Even at the edge of survival, generosity persisted. In 1836, a few years before the storm, the physician William Wilde—father of Oscar Wilde—had visited the island. He wrote of the villages of Keem and Keel:

> "The huts of the inhabitants are all circular or oval, and built for the most part of round, water-washed stones, collected from the beach, and arranged without lime or any other cement, exactly as we have reason to believe that the habitations of the ancient Firbolgs were constructed."[1]

To outsiders, these stone dwellings seemed relics of an ancient past. To islanders, they were lifelines: shelters against wind and sea, homes tied by a central beam.

Inside each Achill cottage, a roof beam known as the cearchall (pronounced car-a-chul) carried the house's weight. From it hung tools, sacred items, even food for safekeeping. It was timber, yes—but also symbol. The cearchall kept the home intact. It bore the strain. It did not break.

By 1911, the island's population had climbed to 6,919 —surpassing pre-famine levels. Yet the recovery would not last. By 1979, numbers had dropped again to under 4,000, the tide of emigration carrying Achill's children outward across the sea.[2]

As I followed Mary's story, I kept returning to that image of the island home—the beam that bore the strain so the rest could stand. To me, Achill is more than backdrop; it is that beam, shaping the character of those who left as much as those who stayed.

Mary embodies the cearchall: the central support of her family, holding them upright through poverty, migration, and loss. Like the houses of her childhood, she endured.

A View of Achill. *The Illustrated London News*, 23 March 1844.

2

THE COLONY: THE PRICE OF SOUP

"The salvation of immortal souls ... was a worthy object for the expenditure of a smaller sum of the world's wealth than is often squandered ... on the follies and vanities of this perishing world."
— Rev. Edward Nangle, *Achill Missionary Herald and Western Witness*

When I began tracing the life of my great-grandmother, I expected the search to take me through the usual parish registers, census returns, and local histories.

What I did not expect was the surprise hidden in her parents' marriage record—a Church of Ireland ceremony. That single detail led me down an unexpected path of research, one that revealed the existence of the Achill Mission, a Protestant settlement whose influence rippled far beyond its borders.

Long before Mary was born beneath the slopes of Slievemore, Achill Island had already been shaped—not by war or conquest, but by faith, and the struggle for it.

In the 1830s, into this remote and weather-hardened place came Reverend Edward Nangle, a fiery evangelical of the Church of Ireland. He saw Achill not merely as impoverished, but as a heathen outpost, spiritually adrift. With the zeal of a revivalist, he cast himself as a soldier in a battle for souls. Backed by English benefactors and the Achill Missionary Society, Nangle set out to "conquer" the island for Christ—not with bayonets, but with Bibles, sermons, and soup.[1]

From 1834, on the windswept shore at Dugort, Nangle planted what he believed was a fortress of the Gospel. By 1835, "the Colony" already had a church, orphanage, hospital, hotel, farmland, workers' cottages, and a printing press. Schools sprang up across the island—in Dugort, Slievemore, Cashel, and Keel, with later ventures in Dooega and Bullsmouth. At one point, in the summer of 1835, there were eight schools in Achill: four Protestant, three Catholic subscription schools, and one old hedge school hanging on.[2]

The Catholic Church did not remain passive. Led by Archbishop John MacHale of Tuam, it called for *exclusive dealing*—a community-wide boycott of the Colony.[3] Islanders were told not to trade with it, not to work for it, and not to send their children to its schools. This wasn't mere rivalry; in tightly bound communities, crossing that line meant risking isolation, even ostracism.

Still, the Colony grew. By the 1840s, it had taken more land at Mweelin and expanded its reach into education, health, and industry. The printing press at Dugort, one of the finest in the west, became Nangle's pulpit on paper—churning out *The Achill Missionary Herald and Western*

Witness, cataloguing each conversion as a victory in an ongoing spiritual crusade.

The famine years brought the Colony its most controversial chapter. While its leaders insisted that relief was given freely, many believed it came with conditions. "Souperism" was the bitter term for taking Protestant aid—especially soup—in exchange for conversion.[4] For some, these were not theological choices but survival decisions, made when the alternative was starvation.

The divide even followed people to the grave. Converts were sometimes buried apart from their neighbours. Families who took aid could carry the stigma for years. Those who returned to Catholicism often did so quietly—through confession or whispered prayers—rather than public renunciation.

When Griffith's Valuation was compiled in 1855, the Mission's influence was recorded in black and white. The Trustees of the Achill Mission held land in Dugort, Keel, Dooega, and Mweelin.[5] Allied landlords like Thomas Brassy and Samuel Holmes—buying up plots from the famine-struck O'Donnell estate via the Encumbered Estates Court—controlled still more. In a place where tenancy meant survival, this was real power.

The Gaughan family's own story was touched by this world. In Church of Ireland baptismal registers, four Gaughans—Mark, Patrick, Antony, and Dominik—are marked "recantation," possibly meaning they had converted from Catholicism. Dominik's wife, Nancy Masterton, is also noted as recanting in 1845.[6] Mission burial records list Gaughan children—Anthony (nine months), Maria (five years), and Kate (twelve years)—all dead between 1847 and 1853.

In 1854, amid this religious tension, Henry Gaughan

married Mary O'Donnell at the Dugort Chapel of Ease—known as St Thomas—which had opened that same year. The service was conducted by Reverend Joseph Barker and witnessed by Reverend John Vickers, both key figures in the Mission.[7] hat single record proved pivotal: it confirmed the unusual setting of their wedding and supplied the names of two of my third-great-grandfathers, Thomas Gaughan and Pat O'Donnell—both recorded in Griffith's Valuation for Dooagh, confirming the family's link to that part of the island.

At the time of Henry and Mary's marriage, registration rules were complicated: civil registration of Protestant marriages had begun in 1845 with the Church of Ireland acting as the official authority, while Catholic marriages were legally recognised if performed by a priest under the Marriage (Ireland) Act 1844; civil registration of all births, deaths and marriages did not begin until 1 January 1864.[8] But where a marriage involved a Protestant—or crossed the religious divide—it usually had to be recorded through the civil system, often via the Church of Ireland. In Henry and Mary's case, this may explain why their wedding appears in the Mission's registers, even if their personal beliefs were more complex.

What we do know is that there is no evidence linking Henry and Mary directly to the Colony. They appear to have remained in Dooagh, a staunchly Catholic village, where they raised their children—Thomas, Mary, Catherine, John, the twins Pat and Martin, Anthony, and Bridget—within the old traditions.

By the time Mary Gaughan was a child, the Colony was already in decline. In 1857—just three years after her parents' marriage—Reverend Edward Nangle's ambitious vision had begun to unravel. He had relocated to Skreen in

THE COLONY: THE PRICE OF SOUP

Co. Sligo and become embroiled in a protracted dispute with the Irish Society for Church Missions, which eventually withdrew its support. By the 1860s, the Colony's once-thriving buildings on Achill were weathering under the Atlantic winds, converts were quietly returning to Catholicism, and attendance at its schools was steadily dwindling.

Yet its shadow still stretched across the island.

A striking case, reported in the *Weekly Register and Catholic Standard* on 3 October 1863, (p. 211) illustrates how agents of the Colony continued to wield power in Dooagh. Notices to quit were served on at least ten families without clear justification. The supposed offence? Pieces of driftwood—planks washed ashore from wrecks—that villagers had taken into their homes. The timber was claimed as Mission property, and those accused were dragged before the Petty Sessions Court. Several men, including James McNamara, Anthony Mangan, Pat McNamara, and Martin Vassy, were sentenced to twelve months' hard labour in Castlebar Gaol. Their eviction warrants soon followed, forcing them to surrender their land to the Mission's agent. Others, equally blameless, suffered the same fate. As the article observed bitterly, honest tenants were being uprooted on the flimsiest of grounds, with every household left vulnerable to the whims of "this Catholic philanthropy of the Gospel and of Gospel-loving men."[9]

By 1882, however, the grand experiment that had once dominated Achill's religious and social life was effectively over.

Debate still lingers over what the Colony truly brought to the island. To some, it was a civilising force—bringing education, medical care, and infrastructure. To others, it was an alien imposition that split neighbours and families, sowing mistrust that endured for generations. When I first encountered the history of the Colony, my mind leapt to modern comparisons: Jim Jones's Jonestown, or the Rajneeshpuram commune in Oregon—movements that sought utopia but bred division. Yet the Achill Mission resists simple comparisons. It certainly put the island on the map, forced the Catholic Church to re-engage with a community it had long neglected, expanded schooling, and even, somewhat paradoxically, supported the Irish language through its publications.

But its impact wasn't confined to buildings or newspapers. Mary would have grown up hearing its story not from textbooks, but from voices—at wakes, by the fire, in the fields. Stories of who had "taken the soup," who had gone, who had come back. Some told with bitterness. Others with quiet understanding. This wasn't distant history—it was living memory, shaping how neighbours saw each other long after the Mission's windows were boarded up and its sermons silenced.

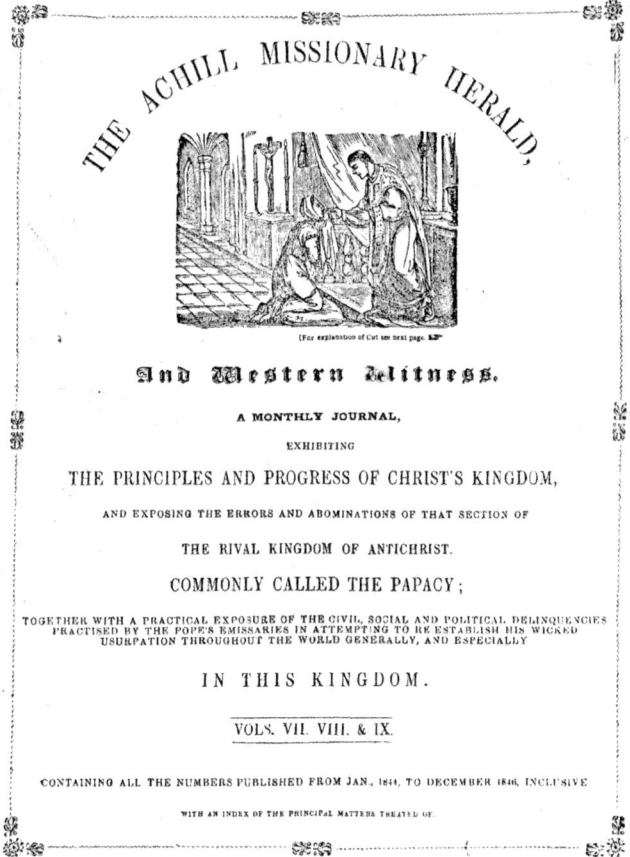

The Achill Missionary Herald, and it's anti-catholic propaganda fully advertised on the front page!

Henry Gaughan's & Mary O'Donnell, marriage certificate Dugort Chapel of Ease (St Thomas) 1854

St Thomas', Dugort (Doogort), Achill Island.

3
DOOAGH: A VILLAGE ON THE EDGE

If the story of Achill in the 1830s and 1840s was shaped by the Colony and its controversies, the story of Mary's family was rooted in Dooagh—a village on the island's far western edge, exposed to the full force of the Atlantic. Within Dooagh, the Gaughans lived in the area known as Keelwest, a scatter of cottages and fields pressed hard against the sea.

Unlike English villages, whose histories can often be traced back to the *Domesday Book*, Irish villages rarely have such continuous documentation.

To understand what life was like in Keelwest during Mary Gaughan's time, you must work with fragments—newspaper reports, court records, and eyewitness accounts. It is less a neat archive than a puzzle: piecing together a world seldom written down but deeply lived.

Dooagh's name derives from Dumha (Dubh) Acha, meaning "mound of the field" or "sandbank."[1] Some suggest the village expanded after the Great Famine, as families moved closer to the coast for access to food. It seems to have taken on a more permanent form after the Land Commission divisions of the 1880s. With formal records scarce, much of its history survives in how others described it.

Outsiders who passed through Achill in the nineteenth century left remarkably consistent impressions. They often mingled pity with disdain, exaggeration with fascination. The *Illustrated London News* (23 March 1844) gave a stark description:

"The island of Achill is washed by the Atlantic Ocean... wild and primitive... huts that do not seem at all to belong to a civilised land... its inhabitants are as rude as its rocky shore...The poor inhabitants live and sleep with their poultry or cattle, glad to be rich enough to own such fellow-lodgers."[2]

Half a century later, little seemed to have changed. A letter to *The Freeman's Journal* in October 1895, under the headline *Desolate Achill*, described Dooagh as a village of "eight hundred souls" living "on the very edge of the Atlantic... the waves dashing with ceaseless roar."[3]

Other reports piled on grimness. The *Farmer's Gazette* painted a picture of "five hundred human beings crowded up in a cluster of stone hovels... filth, untidiness, and general squalid wretchedness... yet troops of merry, healthy-looking children" spilling out to beg or sell amethysts from the mountains.[4]

By 1906, John Harris offered the most detailed portrait. He described Dooagh's cabins as if "shaken out of a gigantic pepper-box," scattered along a trout stream. Inside, he found rags, turf fires, and families crammed with livestock under one roof. He once saw geese, pigs, a cow, a horse, and

DOOAGH: A VILLAGE ON THE EDGE

a whole family emerge from a single windowless cabin. Yet alongside the hardship, he noticed generosity. Islanders responded to the smallest kindness with torrents of blessings:

"The Lord spare thee, give thee long life, and send thee safe in all thy journeys." [5]

To outsiders, it seemed primitive. To islanders, it was simply home. Fires burned constantly, doors faced east against the wind, and even in want, gratitude shaped daily life.

By 1920, Rev. Patrick Joseph Joyce summed it up with a wry phrase in the *Irish Independent*: Dooagh, he said, was "the biggest village in Europe in which the tiniest houses are inhabited by the largest families in Ireland."[6]

All the above descriptions give a realistic sense of Achill and Dooagh in the Gaughans' time. But how did they arrive, and how long had they lived in Dooagh? I hoped to answer those questions.

John McNamara of Keelwest, Dooagh—whom I discovered to be a cousin four times removed—preserved an oral tradition about how the Gaughans first came to Achill:

> "The Gaughans were supposed to have been fishermen from Doohoma, across the bay, who fished the waters behind Slievemore and stayed in huts in Annagh Bay. The fishing grounds there were rich and sheltered. They walked over the mountain heather to the deserted village, became acquainted with the local girls, and some of them stayed and married."

This memory aligns with the records. Aside from Griffith's Valuation and the marriage certificate of Henry Gaughan and Mary O'Donnell, I uncovered other snippets of the Gaughans' presence in Dooagh by trawling newspapers.

An unusual press clipping provides yet another glimpse. The *Mayo Constitution* (24 January 1860) reported under the headline *Longevity in the West*:

> "In the islands of Achill there is living at present time a man named Thomas Gaughan, of Doowagh[*], aged 113. He is hale and hearty, and not long since walked a distance of twenty-four miles. There is also a woman named Gaughan residing at Meelan aged 104."[7]

Whether this Thomas and the Gaughan woman from Meelan (Mweelin) are directly related is uncertain, but the name, place, and timing are telling.

Not all glimpses are flattering.

The Petty Sessions Court Registers add another layer of detail. An entry dated 15 January 1861 not only exposes the tensions running through the community but also places Mary's parents and maternal grandparents squarely at the heart of events. The complaint, lodged by Bartley Gallagher of Dooagh and Slievemore, recounts a Christmas Day clash:

---

[*] The reporter misspelled the name of the village.

> "That on Christmas Day, the 25th of December 1860, after Mass, my wife Mary Gallagher, myself and others went into Anthony Molloy's Public House in Keel... and after having some drink there, James O'Donnell, Pat O'Donnell and Kate O'Donnell... in a violent threatening manner, threatened to assault me. Myself and my wife went home to Dooagh... and in the evening a crowd of persons came to my door in a riotous and disorderly manner... A stone was thrown against my window shutter, and several against the house... I saw Manus O'Donnell, Bryan Patten, Harry Gaughan, John O'Donnell, Michael Lavelle, Mary Gaughan, and others of Dooagh, with sticks and stones in their hands... My wife was struck on the head with a stone... and cried out that she was killed. My wife was very much cut by that blow, and I believe her life to be in danger... She was twice attended by Doctor Carmichael of Achill."[8]

The case was scheduled for 25 January 1861. Two of the accused—Manus O'Donnell and Bryan Patten—were committed to Castlebar Gaol pending a medical certificate. Warrants were issued for the rest.

This episode, preserved in a faded court register, offers a rare glimpse into the social fabric of 1860s Dooagh. In this scene, Harry and Mary Gaughan—my great-great-grandparents—as well as Pat O'Donnell and Kate O'Donnell, Mary's maternal grandparents, step briefly but unmistakably into view. Their inclusion in the complaint confirms that they were not just names in a ledger, but real people in a real community where tensions sometimes boiled over.

It firmly anchors them to a specific time and place, reinforcing the Gaughans' connection to Dooagh. It also reveals a difficult truth about rural Irish life: it was communal and close-knit, but not without conflict.

Whether this hostility carried into later generations is difficult to say. Yet, while searching the Petty Sessions registers for further Gaughan entries, I found that in 1905 two Gallagher brothers from Dugort were charged with assaulting a Patrick Gaughan in Westport. Was it mere coincidence—or the echo of an old grievance passed down like land or lore? Could there have been, in some small way, a Gaughan–Gallagher version of the Joyces and O'Flahertys?[9]

We may never know how the 1861 case ended; the court's conclusion is lost. But what survives—these faded pages of testimony—tells us something human and clear: the Gaughans of Keelwest, Dooagh were real, witnessed, and embedded in a place that shaped them and carried their name forward.

"THE FISHERY. DOUACH. ACHILL. Co. MAYO". Circa 1890. Image credit: Robert French, Lawrence Collection, courtesy of National Library of Ireland.

4

THE ROAD TO PAISLEY

As my research moved into the 1870s, I began finding multiple Gaughan birth records thanks to the introduction of compulsory civil registration. These births were further corroborated by research from the North Mayo Heritage Centre. That research also taught me a valuable lesson: the dates were sometimes inconsistent, primarily because families delayed registering events.

These records brought the family's hardships into sharper focus. Two of Mary Gaughan's siblings died young —Bridget in 1873, aged seven, and Anthony, who lived only two days in 1875. In a village shaped by scarcity and relentless weather, grief was all too familiar.

The Gaughans, like all of Achill, had long known poverty's relentless presence. The Great Famine —*An Gorta Mór*— only intensified a struggle that predated it, as families toiled tirelessly but reaped little reward from the unforgiving land. Fishing, crucial for survival, was especially hazardous in places like Dooagh, where the lack of a formal harbour forced fishermen to launch from a treacherous natural inlet. After Black '47, mere survival demanded innovation and adaptation.

One of the most enduring institutions was the clachan—the small hamlets that clustered in Achill's valleys and on its hillsides. A clachan was more than a group of cottages; it was a web of kinship. Houses were sited close together for shelter from Atlantic winds, and families shared fields, tools, and labour in a cycle of mutual dependence. Life was communal and rarely private, but that closeness forged the resilience that helped people withstand loss and hardship.

Booleying—the seasonal movement of livestock known as transhumance—was central to island life. Each summer, families drove their cattle and sheep from the permanent village fields to the upland pastures of the island's commons, living for weeks in small turf or stone huts while the lowland plots recovered. The custom structured the rhythm of the community: shared grazing rights, cooperative herding, and traditional rules of rotation maintained balance and mutual dependence. It relieved pressure on the island's thin soils and reinforced the deep connection between people, their villages, and the common land. According to historian Theresa McDonald, Achill was the last place in Ireland where booleying survived.

By the time Mary was eleven, her fate was already shaped. Like many of her peers, her path did not lead to a neighbouring village, but across the Irish Sea.

No migration records survive, but based on her age at death and the migration patterns of Achill, Mary likely left around 1878. She may have travelled with her sister Ann and brother Tom, joining the tide of children sent each summer to Scotland to keep their families afloat.

Each year, hundreds of islanders were recruited by local "gaffers," working for Scottish potato merchants who managed their travel, wages, and lodgings. Children—some barely in their teens—joined the ranks of potato pickers scattered across the Scottish Lowlands, in regions like Stirlingshire, Ayrshire, and Renfrewshire. Work ran from June through October. Days were long, back-breaking, and soaked in rain. Workers lived in draughty barns, crude bothies, or overcrowded rooms, often with strangers.

Joyce's 1910 account gives a grim picture of the conditions many endured. Quoting a government inspection of Irish fruit pickers in Blairgowrie, he wrote:

"The accommodation afforded them was pronounced 'wretched and demoralizing.' In one very small compartment slept fourteen persons from Achill, ten men and four girls, feet to feet, the men on one side and the girls on the other. Cut away from this by a wooden partition, seven feet high, in about the same amount of space, slept a large number of tramp labourers, whose language and conduct was described as fearful. The beds consisted of a little straw, spread on a few plank boards, with a small, light blanket, which they had to carry about from place to place to cover them."[1]

Though written in 1910, it likely reflects what Mary endured decades earlier. If conditions were unacceptable in Joyce's time, they were surely no better in the 1870s. Still, Achill migrants adapted. Those working on remote farms lodged on-site. Those near towns often found rooms—perhaps explaining why so many Gaughans settled in Paisley.

While most workers returned to Achill each winter, records don't tell us when—or if—Mary went back. A Poor Law entry from 1886 notes that she had "come from Ireland eight years ago," yet she does not appear in the 1881 census for Scotland or England. It's possible she returned to Dooagh, or that she was simply missed from the census.

Her brother Tom seemed more settled. By the early 1880s, he had married Bridget Patten*, another Achill native, and settled in Paisley—by that stage it was a thriving industrial town where many Irish migrants found steady work in the textiles mills. Their daughter Ann was born in July 1885. Tom, listed as a general labourer, had broken free from seasonal work. By 1887, the family was on West Street, where their son Henry (Harry) was born. Tom was now working as a railway labourer—hard work, but more secure than the fields.

Ann, the eldest sister, eventually settled in West Lothian. Her life remained bound to the rhythm of seasonal labour, but she, too, followed the well-worn path of Achill migrants. In 1890, she became pregnant by Anthony McGowan, a shale miner born in Linlithgow to Irish parents. The diaspora was spreading—but remained close-knit.

Mary's path was harsher. By 1883, she had met a young man recorded as "Pat Lees" in Poor Law records—likely Peter Lees, a 20-year-old carter listed in Paisley's 1881 census. Still in her teens, Mary became pregnant.

Why she and Lees never married remains unknown. Later records described her as "deserted." He may have left, or perhaps the weight of poverty made marriage impossible.

---

* The family name appears with varying spellings in historical records, including Patton, Paton, and Patten.

Whatever the truth, the evidence suggested that Mary faced the road ahead alone.

After giving birth, Mary remained in or near Paisley, where she had family connections. Poor Law records mention a relative—Catherine Patten, her sister-in-law Bridget's sister—who lived at 30 King Street with her fiancé, Bernard (Bryan) Patten. It appears that Mary returned to seasonal work, though raising a child while labouring in the fields would have been nearly impossible. Eventually—and likely in a moment of painful necessity—she left her infant daughter, also named Mary, in the care of Jane Caldwell, a woman who lived on the same street.

A Poor Law entry dated 30 September 1886 captures her plight with blunt precision:

"This woman states she was born in Co Mayo, can't tell her age, came from Ireland 8 years ago. She promises to send money while working away. Caldwell promises to keep child, working in Stirlingshire, Ayrshire, Kilbride, Mearns, Lounsdale, Paisley & all over the County of Renfrew."[2]

It was desperate, but not uncommon. Many migrant women were forced into similar arrangements to survive.

The child was baptised at St Mirin's Church on 21 February 1884, when Mary was living at 149 George Street, Paisley. Pat Lees was not named on the baptismal record, and the only witness was recorded as "Mrs Ferguson." I have never found any connection to this Mrs Ferguson, and she was almost certainly not a relation.

Tragedy soon followed. Records place Mary at 10

Guildry Court, in Glasgow's Bridgegate district—known locally as the Briggait—by the autumn of 1886. It was an area long associated with poverty, overcrowding, and crime. That same season, her infant daughter died of whooping cough on 27 November 1886. The event is noted only in the death register: no obituary, no headstone, no surviving record beyond a single entry. Just a name, a date—and silence.

In that same bleak season, Mary met John Gorman—the man who would become my great-grandfather.

Tracing John Gorman's birth proved testing. I first found a John born in 1849 in Tarbolton, Ayrshire whose parental details matched my records. But when I traced his sister Sarah Ann the picture became confusing: by 1855 Sarah Gorman (their mother) had eight children by age thirty-eight, with a son and a daughter already deceased. A Sarah Ann born in 1850 died in 1853, and another daughter named Sarah Ann was born later that year. The confusion deepened when I uncovered a 1858 birth in Ireland—registered at St Mirin's in Paisley, Scotland—naming John Gorman with the same parents. That 1858 John was my great-grandfather, which suggests the John born in 1849 had died before 1855.

John Gorman was a journeyman shoemaker, the son of Henry Gormal (later Gorman) of Madden parish, Armagh, and Sarah Daly of Rowan, Derrynoose, Armagh —Irish agricultural labourers who crossed sectarian lines to marry in Keady before starting life together in Scotland.

The Gormans first appear in the 1851 Scottish Census, recorded on High Street, Irvine, where Henry is listed as an "earthenware dealer." Between 1851 and 1861, the family moved from Irvine to New Cumnock and eventually settled in Pudding Lane, Paisley, by which time their surname had evolved to "Gorman."

Henry died of bronchitis in 1861, leaving Sarah to raise their children in the crowded slums of Paisley. My great-grandfather's early years appear to have been marked by instability, and his working life reflected that: initially trained as a lithographer, he later turned to shoemaking—travelling door to door with his tools, a tradesman whose livelihood depended on the next knock.

On John Gorman's 1858 birth record, one witness is listed as "Catherine Gaughan," which may hint at how John and Mary first connected, though that remains speculative. What I can say is that they most likely met at 8 King Street, where John was registered in July 1886—the same month Sarah applied for poor relief. Their bond, forged in poverty and shared struggle, deepened quickly. By January 1887 they were living together in a single room at 12 Merchant Lane, near the Briggait, and that month Mary gave birth to their son Henry, named for both their fathers.

One useful feature of Scottish birth registers is that they provide the parents' marriage date. In the 1887 birth record of Henry Gorman, a date is given for John and Mary's marriage—19 February 1886, Paisley. However, no official record of this union exists, and whether they formally married remains uncertain. Coincidentally, this was the exact date of Tom's documented marriage to Bridget Patten a year earlier. The reused date may have been borrowed to lend respectability, or perhaps no formal wedding ever took place. For people living on the margins, survival often mattered more than ceremony.

What is clear is this: Mary Gaughan was no longer just the girl from Dooagh. She had become a mother, a worker, and a survivor in Glasgow's roughest quarters.

I began to trace her journey along a jagged arc—from the stone cottages of Achill, to the furrowed fields of Renfrewshire, and on to the soot-blackened lanes of Glasgows Clydeside.

Yet Mary's story was far from unique. The records reveal a broader pattern: hundreds of men and women from Achill made the same seasonal crossings to Scotland each year, seeking wages in the fields that might sustain their families through winter. Her experience fits within this wider system of economic necessity and migration that linked Achill to the agricultural counties of western Scotland. To understand Mary's life fully, it must be viewed not in isolation, but as part of this recurring movement of people whose survival depended on the rhythm of the harvest.

5

THE MACHINERY OF MIGRATION

Mary's story was one thread in a much larger tapestry of hardship and movement—one that bound generations of Achill families to the fields of Scotland. The annual migration of islanders, known colloquially as *tattie-hoking*, shaped not only individual lives but entire communities. Though Mary's journey revealed its human cost, the broader system deserves a closer look: the routes they followed, the debts they repaid, and the resilience they carried into the damp furrows of Ayrshire and Stirlingshire.

While men from Achill also took part in the potato harvests, it was often the women and children who drew the most attention in newspaper reports of the late nineteenth and early twentieth centuries. The squalid bothies where they lived—cramped huts with no privacy, little sanitation, and poor ventilation—shocked Victorian and Edwardian readers accustomed to the order of municipal housing schemes.

On the Scottish census, they were recorded as outdoor workers, agricultural labourers, or simply labourers, but locally they became known as *tattie-howkers*. The very word *howking* sounds coarse to modern ears, yet in Scotland it carried a simple meaning—"howking" meant to dig or to search.[1]

For Achill migrants, it meant weeks of relentless labour in damp, cold furrows, often on remote Scottish farms. Many of the youngest worked from before sunrise to well after dusk—rising at three in the morning and toiling until seven at night, backs bent low in the fields. Breaks were short, the work endless, the pay meagre. And yet, the few pounds earned during those months could mean the difference between hunger and survival through the long winter.

The roots of this annual exodus stretched back to the aftermath of the Great Famine, when Achill's *clachan* settlements evolved into migrant-based communities. As described in Mary's childhood, the *clachan* was a network of kinship and cooperation, and from these same hamlets the summer squads were formed. Each household sent at least one young worker—usually between thirteen and twenty-three—across the water, travelling in groups under the supervision of a foreman or gaffer. What began as a desperate response to hunger hardened over decades into a recurring rhythm of life.

Underlying the system was debt—a recurring burden for island families. Much of it was incurred during the winter months, when goods were bought on credit to see them through. Newspapers of the time recorded how islanders often paid inflated prices compared with mainland markets, locking them into a cycle of arrears. When the potato crop failed at home, repayment was impossible without wages earned abroad. Seasonal migration became a necessity, and the youngest members of each household bore the heaviest share of that burden.

THE MACHINERY OF MIGRATION

Achill's migration was not unique. Families from Donegal and Connaught also travelled for seasonal work, carving out their own routes. Achill islanders mainly went to western Scotland, Donegal workers gravitated east, and Connaught families often moved into Northumberland. Some travelled further south to pick corn or beet. The work was grinding, the conditions primitive, but the routes became ritualised. Mothers led children onto steamers bound for Greenock, cousins reunited in the fields, and neighbours endured hardship side by side.

By modern standards, both the living and working conditions were tantamount to slave labor.[2] Yet they did not go unchallenged. In 1900, the Departmental Committee on Migratory Labourers from Ireland to Scotland heard testimony from Mary O'Donnell of Achill, aged eighteen:

"I am 18 years of age. I have been to Scotland to work for four successive years, and my sister, aged 16, has been twice. Last year I went in May with my father, sister, and brother, aged 14, and we all worked on the same farm. My father was the 'gaffer,' and looked after 27 girls and 13 boys. We were first weeding on a farm near Paisley and all slept in the town. I was paid 2s a day. The men paid 2s 6d a week for lodgings, and the girls 1s. The men's food cost them about 8s a week. The girls' food cost about 5s a week. We then went to Ayrshire, potato digging on a farm for six weeks. We slept in a barn there. The men had one and the girls another. Sometimes when we were in Ayrshire we began work at 3 a.m. and left off at 2 p.m. When we did this we worked as follows: Began work 3 a.m., stopped work 8 a.m. for breakfast. We stopped again at 11 a.m. for a quarter of an hour and took a piece of loaf, and we knocked off work at 2 p.m. The rest of the day we played about and went to bed about 5 or 6 p.m. The ordinary hours are from 7 a.m. to 6 p.m. At 9.30 we have a quarter of an hour off, at 12 o'clock an hour off, and at 4 p.m. a quarter of an hour off. For breakfast they used to give us tea, white bread, butter, and eggs. For dinner, 3 p.m., we either had fish or meat. The girls got 13s 6d a week. My brother got 15s a week. Some cousins of mine, boys, got £1 a week each. After this we went to Stirlingshire. At the harvest the men are paid 5s a day and girls 4s. For a month's harvest a man gets about £4 and his food and bed. A woman gets £3 and her food and bed. We buy our clothes in Scotland."[3]

Irish MPs later raised questions in the House of Commons[4], and in 1918, when many seasonal workers refused to travel, a committee was formed to negotiate better wages and conditions. The Achill workers were represented by Michael Masterton, presumed to be a leading 'gaffer' from the island. While the Glasgow Trades Council pledged improvements, progress was limited and largely superficial.[5]

The tragic consequences of neglect were laid bare on 16 September 1937, when ten young Achill men—members of a tattie-hoking squad in Kirkintilloch—died after their bothy filled with toxic fumes. The horror of their deaths shocked the nation and finally brought the plight of Ireland's migratory workers into full public view.

As a reaction to the Kirkintilloch tragedy, the Irish government established a committee to investigate how it might improve the conditions under which Achill workers were employed.

By November 1938, the Éire Inter-Departmental Committee delivered its findings. Its conclusion was bleak it stated that it was:

> "unable to suggest any effective means which the Government of this country could bring about any improvement in the conditions under which the Achill workers are employed."

In other words, the committee claimed that it could do little. Responsibility, it suggested, rested with the workers themselves, who would have to confront the exploitation of the *gaffer* system on their own.

The committee went further, making clear that:

> "the provision of suitable housing accommodation of the workers while they are employed in Great Britain is a matter within the jurisdiction of the United Kingdom."

In short, Dublin was unwilling—or unable—to intervene directly in Scotland.

Yet the committee did make one striking proposal, which in my view bordered on the radical. In order to reduce dependence on migration, it suggested keeping workers at home through "a scheme of land-settlement, industrial development and re-afforestation."

The plan was vast in scale. It proposed relocating 6,000 families from Achill and other congested districts—amounting to almost one-third of the total area of Éire—and resettling them on 150,000 acres of untenanted land elsewhere in the country. This would mean nothing less than the forced re-location of Achill families from their ancestral homes.[6]

One could argue that government intervention was necessary, but relocation was not the answer. For Mary's people, tattie-howking was more than seasonal labour—it was, I believe, part of the island's inheritance, a rhythm carried in motion. Neighbours travelled together, families were bound by necessity, and songs and stories echoed across damp furrows. I think it shaped their sense of self as much as it sustained their bodies. What began as survival grew into a shared identity—marked by resilience, sacrifice, and the unspoken bond of hardship endured together. My belief is reinforced by evidence that seasonal potato work from Mayo persisted well beyond the early twentieth century: RTÉ documentary material and newsreel show Irish pickers in Scotland in the 1950s–1970s, and Anne O'Dowd's landmark study records interview testimony of men and women from Ballina and Mulranny still doing tattie-howking in the 1980s.[7]

Even the testimony of Mary O'Donnell in 1900—quite possibly a cousin of my great-grandmother, since O'Donnell was her mother's maiden name—echoes this same inheritance. Her words sit within that longer tradition of endurance, reminding us that the families of Achill were never separate threads but part of a tightly woven fabric.

Tattie Howkers, Ayrshire, circa 1890s - Reproduced by kind permission of Kenny Baird (Ayrshire History). Photograph from the John Clark Madison collection.

6

SHADOWS OVER ACHILL

While Mary Gaughan was carving out a life in the soot-darkened closes of Glasgow's Briggait, the world she had left behind on Achill Island carried on at its own steady rhythm. From the cliffs of Croaghaun to the tide-washed shore of Dooagh, life still revolved around turf and tide, Mass and memory. Fires glowed in hearths, the wind slipped between cottages, carrying news, grief, and the soft weight of stories.

In the late 1880s, Mary's brother Tom returned to Achill with his wife, Bridget, and their two children, Ann and Harry. They lodged first with Bridget's family in Bun an Churraigh (Bunacurry), a village nestled between hill and lake. There, two more children—Patrick and Mary—were added to the household.

But loss soon struck. In the winter of 1890, their father, Harry, died at sixty-five. His life in Dooagh is faintly recorded: a fleeting mention in the 1860 Petty Sessions, a marriage certificate naming him a labourer, a death entry calling him a "Farmer & Fisherman."[1] Like many Achill men, he may have balanced small farming with fishing—

netting herring, salmon, or turbot, perhaps tending a "free parcel" of land divided by the Land Commission. The records remain silent, leaving only glimpses. His death was registered by the youngest son, John, who soon joined the tide of Achill youth crossing the water as tattie-hokers.

By 1893, John was employed on a farm in Stirlingshire, where he met Lizzie Crossley, an outdoor worker from Girvan whose family had a long seafaring background. They married in 1896 and welcomed a son, another Henry, the following year.

Meanwhile, Tom and Bridget's marriage faltered. In May 1893, Bridget applied for poor relief in Paisley, reporting that Tom had deserted her in Dooagh.[2] At the same time, the Dublin–Westport railway was being extended toward Achill.[3] Tom, who had worked as a railway labourer in Scotland, may have seized the chance to return to the trade. Whatever the reason for his disappearance, it was not permanent—he later reappears alongside the family in Dooagh.

The extension of the railway to Achill appeared to offer new opportunities for connection, yet it would soon be associated with one of the island's darkest chapters.

On 14 June 1894, hundreds gathered at Darby's Point in Cloughmore for the annual crossing to Scotland's potato fields. A poor harvest had left families in debt, and every able-bodied youth was needed to earn. The *Victory*, a wooden hooker, was the first boat to depart, crowded with more than 120 passengers. As it approached the SS *Elm* in Westport Quay, many rushed to one side for a better view. A sudden gust caught the sails. The boat capsized instantly.

Panic followed. Some were trapped beneath the heavy canvas, others pulled under by the crush of bodies. Two local boys, Daniel Burke and Edward O'Malley, dragged several to safety. O'Malley later recalled seeing faces beneath the sail—bloated and helpless, "like footballs."[4]

Thirty-two drowned, most from the Valley and neighbouring villages. Among them were three sisters—Mary, Margaret, and Ann Malley—and twelve-year-old Mary McFarland, returning to Glasgow after visiting her family in Tonragee. The dead were laid out in a Westport cargo shed. Though the Achill railway had not officially opened, a special train carried the coffins and survivors back to the island.

For many, the disaster seemed the fulfilment of a prophecy long attributed to Red Brian Carabine, a Mayo seer:

> "Carriages on wheels, with smoke and fire, will come to Achill—and the first and last carriages will carry dead bodies."[5]

The prophecy proved hauntingly true. In June 1894, the first train to Achill carried the drowned. In 1937 came the second fulfilment, when the ten Achill boys who perished in the Kirkintilloch bothy fire were returned home by rail.

The victims of the Clew Bay Disaster were buried in Kildavnet Cemetery, beneath the shadow of Grace O'Malley's ruined tower. The *Mayo News* described the funeral:

> "The whole countryside was black with people. The cries which rent the air and the whole scene generally was appalling... As each coffin was

removed, Mr. Grey Jnr announced the name on the lid, and this was followed by a cry of woe from the respective knot of relatives... A thick mist had begun to fall. As the first shovelful of earth fell upon the coffins the rain fell more heavily and a fierce storm arose. And the wind shrieking over the mountainside and along the valleys of Achill seemed to wave in sympathy with the poor sorrow-laden islanders."[6]

For Achill families, the disaster was not only an isolated calamity but also a warning. Migration offered wages and survival, but at terrible risk. The sea that promised passage could just as easily take it away.

While grief echoed across Achill, Mary's siblings continued to forge fragile futures. Her sister Kate worked near Linlithgow, lodging with her sister Ann McGowan. There she met quarryman John Donnelly, whom she married in 1894. Within two years he was dead of tuberculosis, leaving Kate a widow with three daughters—Nellie, Mary, and Kate—whom she brought back to Dooagh. It was a familiar pattern: widowed daughters returning home to care for parents while raising children of their own.

Tom and Bridget, too, eventually returned to Dooagh. Bridget bore at least nine children, including Ann, Harry, John, Pat, Tom, Julia, Kate, Mary, and an infant Bridget who died young. But hardship did not relent. In 1901, Tom died after a year-long struggle with broncho-pneumonia, his death registered by his teenage son Harry. Bridget herself died in 1904, leaving the younger children to find their way as best they could.

Ann, Tom's eldest daughter, worked in East Lothian,

where she gave birth to two illegitimate children: a son, James, in 1909, and a daughter, Annie, in 1912, who died in infancy. She married Patrick Fadian in 1915, but their marriage was marked by poverty. Records indicate that both were convicted of neglecting her son James and were briefly imprisoned in Calton Jail. James was subsequently placed in care and does not appear to have been returned to them.[7]

Mary, the youngest of Tom and Bridget's children, found work as a waitress in Rosyth. But her life was cut short by tuberculosis in 1917, one more Achill migrant claimed by poverty and disease.

By the early 1900s, Mary Gaughan had lost both of her parents and, it appears, several siblings. Of the twins, Pat and Martin, the latter cannot be traced beyond early records and may have died in infancy or childhood. As for Pat, a death registration for a "Pat Gaughan" recorded in Dooagh in 1895 may pertain to him, although the stated age does not correspond precisely with expectations. Such inconsistencies were not uncommon in rural record-keeping, where recollection often substituted for literacy in the reporting of vital events. The surviving evidence does not establish certainty, but rather outlines a fragmentary and inconclusive record.

The Gaughans' story in these years reflects a pattern of dispersal, hardship, and endurance characteristic of many Achill families. Some members remained in Dooagh, maintaining a tenuous hold on the land; others crossed to Scotland in search of seasonal or industrial work. A few established stability through marriage, employment, or kinship networks, while many others succumbed to poverty, illness, or the hazards of migration.

For families such as the Gaughans—divided between Achill and Glasgow—the closing decades of the nineteenth century were marked by both continuity and disruption. The legacy of migration permeated their choices and shaped their fates, leaving a record defined as much by absence and uncertainty as by survival.

A Newspaper illustration of the "lamentable" Clew Bay tragedy.
Penny Illustrated Paper, 23 June 1894.

7

THE GARNGAD

In the shadow of Glasgow Cathedral, not far from the old Molendinar Burn where monks once drew water and murmured prayers, another district rose—not shaped by devotion, but by the fumes of industry and the struggle to survive. This was the Garngad.

The Garngad was no accident. It was carved into being by migration and Glasgow's insatiable industry. In the 1780s, Irish navvies dug the Monkland Canal, a coal artery into the city. Then came the chemical men, the steelworkers, and the mill women. By the mid-19th century, famine and empire had driven families from Mayo, Sligo, and Donegal into its smoke.

Into this mix came Mary and John Gorman. The reason for their move from Paisley to the Garngad remains uncertain; while family connections to Glasgow existed, by 1888 John's mother and sister were already living in the city, one in the Gorbals and another in Blackfriars, but no clear link to this particular district has been identified. Their relocation may have been prompted by employment—low-paid labour at the St Rollox Chemical Works drew many workers from Ayrshire. Whatever the cause, by the close of the century the Gormans had joined the swelling ranks of the Irish working poor in one of Glasgow's most squalid areas.

Amid soot-blackened brick and the screech of iron, Mary bore the rest of her children: John in 1889, Annie in 1891, Isabella (Bella) in 1893, James in 1895, and William —my grandfather—in 1902, at 105 Garngadhill. Between those years, grief struck twice: two infant sons, both named Thomas, died in 1897 and 1900.

Each child seemed to bring another move—Merchant Lane, Millburn, Street, Middleton Place, Rosemount Street —until they settled at 105 Garngadhill, a cramped two-room house. Conditions changed little: the air thick with chemical dust, walls sweating with damp, the reek of the gasworks seeping through cracked panes. A "home" might mean one room shared by several families. Toilets were outside. Children slept in drawers, under beds, or stairwells —on straw if they were lucky.

Above it all loomed Tennant's Stalk—known locally as Tennant's Lum. Completed in 1842, it towered higher than any chimney in Europe, venting the fumes of the St Rollox Chemical Works, then the largest in the world. Bleaching powder, caustic soda, sulphuric acid—its products travelled the globe, but its poisons lingered close. The canal ran black; the air scorched throats; the soil lay burned and bare. Work at St Rollox or the nearby Tharsis Sulphur Works was punishing—sixty hours a week for pennies. Acid ate through clothes, lungs rotted from fumes, and the Royal Infirmary filled with men coughing blood. Yet the Irish kept coming, driven by need and bound by solidarity.

Historian Iain R. Mitchell, in *Orange, Green and Red: Class, Community and Conflict on Clydeside*, captures a contemporary view of St Rollox and its workers from 1847 through the words of a first-hand witness:

> "The heaps of sulphur, lime, coal and refuse; the intense heat of the scores of furnaces in which the processes are going on; the smoke and thick vapours which dim the air of most of the buildings...the acrid fumes of sulphur and the various acids which worry the eyes, and tickle the nose and choke the throat."

In the 1911 census, the Gormans were recorded at 236 Garngadhill—five of them sharing a single tenement flat. Moving, or "flitting," between flats and houses seems to have been a recurring pattern for the family, likely driven by the constant struggle to meet the rent. Although all the children were in employment, John, the second son, earned his living as a cattle drover at the Moore Street slaughterhouse. Bella and James worked long hours in the local potteries, while William was still a schoolboy.

But three names were missing from the record: Mary's husband, John; her eldest son, Henry; and her daughter, Annie. Their absence was no clerical slip—it held a story of its own, one that would surface later.

Not long after, tragedy struck again. In 1912, Bella gave birth to an illegitimate son, James. His life was heartbreakingly short—he died in January 1913 from pneumonia, barely a year old. In that loss, Bella's story mirrored her mother's: both women had faced the loneliness of raising a child without a father present, and both had endured the devastating grief of a young life lost too soon.

Accounts of the Garngad portray a district of sharp

contrasts—housing conditions among the poorest in Glasgow, yet community ties remarkably strong. Women passed stovies over close railings, and children watched over one another in the shared spaces of the closes. The rosary travelled from flat to flat. St Roch's School educated the Catholic youth of the district, while nearby St Rollox served their Protestant neighbours. Sectarian tensions did arise, particularly during the 1920s, but for most families the struggle to make ends meet outweighed divisions of faith.

Newspapers from the 1880s to the 1930s reported a familiar pattern of Saturday-night disturbances in the Garngad, often ignited when police arrested someone for breach of the peace. Crowds gathered, confronting officers and attempting to free those detained. Bottles, stones, and even handfuls of mud were thrown in chaotic scenes that helped forge the area's reputation. Local personalities and gangs emerged—men such as "Noble Ned" (Dan Kennedy), and groups like the "Muldoon Boys" and the "Romeo Boys." Outsiders, including members of the Scottish Protestant League, added their own insult, nicknaming the locals: "the Garngad Goths."

Yet despite its notoriety, others saw something deeper. As one writer observed: "Even the chemicals could not bleach the humanity from the Garngad."

Industry was both lifeblood and killer. The Tennants grew rich in Grosvenor Square and country estates while their exploited tenants shivered in cold, dark rooms. The workers gave their lives to acid, bleach, soap, and steel. Still, beauty remained. From Garngadhill's summit, you could see the Campsies—and on a clear day, Arran. Beneath the black smoke, a pulse still beat.

"The Good and the Bad"—that was the name locals gave it, and it fit. Whether describing the belching chimneys, the black canal, or the crowded closes, one theme ran through every account: endurance. Not the romantic kind, but the day-to-day kind. Meals stretched to feed an extra mouth. A prayer said for the missing. A child kept warm with a story when blankets ran out. Endurance was the unseen framework holding it all up.

By 1930, city officials sought to rebrand the district as "Royston"—a polished name for a place they deemed unclean. But the old name refused to die, carried with stubborn pride by those who called it home. Garngad—part Gaelic, part industrial, entirely Irish in spirit. Outsiders dismissed it as "the Irish slum," yet inside its crumbling tenements and sulphur-scented streets, people built lives from little more than hard work and hope. To them, it was simply "Little Ireland." Even today, some still call Royston the Garngad—and if proof is needed, there's a pub that bears the name, and it is usually painted green, and white!

Amid poverty, illness, and widowhood, it was women like Mary Gaughan and families like the Gormans who gave the Garngad its character. Their labour filled its factories, their faith steadied its streets, and their endurance stitched its community together. The history of the Garngad is not written in factory records or council reports, but in the lives they built with quiet strength and grace.

ROW IN GARNGAD.

POLICEMEN ROUGHLY HANDLED BY A MOB.

"Noble Dan," otherwise Dan Kennedy, was among the well-known figures who appeared at St. Rollox Court, Glasgow, yesterday, in connection with a row which threatened to assume the proportions of a riot in Garngad Road on Saturday night. "The Road" was in a ferment, and at one time there was a crowd of several hundreds around the police, at whom bottles and other missiles were thrown.

The disturbance was started by Patrick Kelly, who had been refused admission to a public-house. Two constables advised him to go away, but he resented the interference and assaulted one of the officers, knocking him down. The crowd soon gathered, and the police were roughly handled. Word was sent to St. Rollox, and a batch of additional constables, on their arrival had to undergo a similar fusilade of all the handy articles that the people of "The Road" could requisition. Many of the officers were badly injured, one having his hand bitten in the melee, and another unfitted for duty.

At the Court Kelly was sentenced to 30 days' imprisonment, Bailie Guest remarking that policemen had dangerous and arduous enough duties "up there" without being aggravated by characters like him.

"Noble Dan" was detained so that further inquiry may be made into his connection with the row.

Edward Rice, who was convicted of assaulting a constable, was sent to prison for 30 days, while Patrick M'Ateer forfeited a pledge of 21s, having failed to appear.

THE GARNGAD RIOTS.

Sentences on Some of the Accused at St. Rollox Police Court.

The "Paddy" riot, which took place in Garngad Road on Saturday, 1st August, was again in evidence at the St. Rollox Police Court yesterday. The first case called was that of William Bradley, a young man, who was charged with assaulting a man named John Paton by striking him on the face with a stone. Paton's injuries, it appeared, had been rather serious. Bradley denied having thrown the stone, but Police-Judge Martin found the assault proved, and imposed a fine of £2 2s, with the alternative of 30 days' imprisonment. Three lads and a young woman next appeared on a charge of having conducted themselves in a riotous and disorderly manner by cursing and swearing and throwing stones. Pleas of not guilty having been given, evidence was given by several policemen, who stated that the accused, along with others, used party terms and threw stones at the windows of houses occupied by Orangemen. Police-Judge Martin did not think the evidence was strong enough to convict, and found the charge not proven.

Thereafter James Romeo, a half-caste, and Patrick Daw, both about 20 years of age, were charged with a similar offence, alleged to have been committed in Charles Street on Sunday, 2nd August. Both pleaded not guilty, and were defended by Mr. Richardson, writer. Evidence of a protracted nature was given. For the prosecution, it was stated that the accused, along with a number of boys, paraded Garngad Road playing tin whistles. The most of the "bandsmen" were Catholics, and the demonstration was intended as a sort of "set off" to that given by the Orangemen the previous day. Stones were thrown at several windows, and the imprecations uttered against Orangemen were loud and strong.

For the defence Mr. Richardson examined

8

WAR COMES TO ROSEMOUNT STREET

Reading between the lines, I came to see my great-aunt Annie Gorman as a quiet echo of her mother's resilience. Women of her generation, raised in the rhythm of working-class life, were expected to carry both the bread and the burden. It was a familiar path: marry, bear children, keep the home. Like so many young women of the Garngad, Annie joined the pottery works—a trade that demanded patience, dexterity, and stamina.

In 1910, she married Charles "Charlie" Nicholson at St Mungo's Catholic Church. Charlie, an army reservist and galvaniser's labourer, came from a family rooted in Co. Armagh and worked at the nearby Hydepark Motor Works. Their marriage brought together two threads of Glasgow's Irish Catholic diaspora—both shaped by poverty, perseverance, and the inherited stories of a homeland left behind.

The newlyweds settled at 286 Garngadhill, just a few doors from Mary's flat. In the tenements of the Garngad, proximity was a kind of protection. Doors stayed open to family. Children drifted between households. Gossip, grief, and comfort passed across wash lines. Affection was quiet but constant.

Then, in August 1914, everything changed. Britain declared war on Germany, and Charlie, like so many others, was among the first reservists called up. He joined the 8th Battalion of the Gordon Highlanders and was sent to the Western Front—into the bloodied mud of trench warfare.

In autumn 1915, Charlie's battalion was ordered into the Battle of Loos, hurled against the fortified Hohenzollern Redoubt. It was brutal work: bayonets in narrow trenches, grenades in waterlogged mud, men swallowed by the earth itself. On 25 September the 8th Gordons briefly pushed past the Redoubt, taking key positions under heavy fire. But the cost was enormous. German counterattacks forced a retreat, and many were left behind, Charlie among them. His body was never recovered.

Annie was twenty-four. Her marriage ended not with a quarrel, but with a telegram.

Charlie's name is now etched into the Loos Memorial in northern France, alongside more than 20,000 British soldiers with no known grave. Carved in pale Portland stone, it stands as one of the few traces of a young man from the Garngad who left quietly and never came home.

To Annie and Charlie's family, that name—fixed in stone—was all that remained. But I don't think Charlie was ever forgotten. Annie would have kept his memory alive through small gestures—a prayer at Mass, perhaps—and by the simple fact that she never removed her wedding ring.

Charlie's death was only the beginning. In my research, I uncovered—one by one—the ways Mary's sons entered the war.

By 1914, Mary's eldest son, Henry, had already been in uniform for a decade. He enlisted in 1904 with the

Cameronians, which explains his absence from the 1911 census. Initially a reservist, he transferred to the regular army in 1906. Serving with the Queen's Own Cameron Highlanders, he was posted first to Dublin, then much farther afield—to Hong Kong, to Tientsin in northern China, still unsettled in the aftermath of the Boxer Rebellion, and finally to Poona in India. From the regimental magazines I consulted online, his days abroad appear to have been filled with parades, patrols, and the routines of garrison life—an existence worlds away from the smoke and struggle of the Garngad.

When war broke out in 1914, Henry's battalion was sent first to France and later to Salonika, where they fought the Bulgarians. By 1919, he was invalided home—sick and exhausted—to Birkenhead Military Hospital. He never left the army entirely, remaining in the reserves until 1925—a career almost certainly prolonged by the war.

Mary's second son, John, enlisted in 1915. He served with the Argyll and Sutherland Highlanders before transferring to the Seaforths. He was wounded that same year—possibly at Loos, where his brother-in-law had fallen. Discharged in 1918, he came home carrying scars that went beyond the physical.

James, younger still, also enlisted. He served first with the King's Own Scottish Borderers, then transferred to the Seaforth Highlanders—perhaps to be near his brother. Sent to France in 1915, he remained there until 1919, returning with the resilience of youth but carrying the shadow of years spent in the trenches.

Even Mary's youngest daughter, Isabella, could not escape the war's reach. She married James Owens in October 1914, and within weeks he had enlisted. Their daughter, Annie, was born that December, just as he was sent to France. He survived, but records indicate that he returned home in poor health—dysentery and strain leaving him permanently weakened. He was discharged with a pension in 1919.

Somehow, all three of Mary's sons survived—a rare outcome compared with many families of the time. They must have returned changed: perhaps more disciplined, perhaps scarred, or simply worn down—but alive. Only Annie's husband, Charlie, was lost.

It is hard to imagine what Mary endured during those years: three sons at the front, a son-in-law killed, a daughter widowed, and a husband absent from records, his whereabouts unknown. It would have broken many, yet my great-grandmother seemed made of sterner stuff.

Scouring the newspapers for reports of Armistice celebrations in the Garngad revealed nothing. The only article I found was a brief notice of Charlie's death in the *Glasgow Evening Times*. The war may have ended, but the streets were the same—narrow, damp, unforgiving. The men returned to shuttered factories, overcrowded flats, and the silence of missing faces. Grief clung to the tenements like smoke from the gasworks.

Perhaps events unfolding in Ireland during the war years also left their mark on the Garngad?

Pte Charles Nicholson, 8th Service Bn Gordon
Highlanders - From the Evening Times Roll of Honour
(20 Oct 1915) - Glasgow Life, Mitchell Library

AI enhanced image of Charles Nicholson

Henry Gorman's Barracks in Tientsin (China), circa 1906.

9
BEYOND THE HORIZON

When the guns of August 1914 echoed across Europe, Achill Island—perched on Ireland's Atlantic edge—seemed far from the front lines. Yet even its isolation could not keep the Great War at bay. Men from Achill enlisted, and some never returned.

Lieutenant Richard Brinsley Sheridan of Dugort was killed in March 1916 while serving with the 8th Battalion, Dublin Fusiliers. Private Joe Gallagher from Achill Sound died in 1917 with the Connaught Rangers. That same year, Thomas Lendrum, who had emigrated, fell in action with the Australian Army. Their bodies were buried on foreign soil, but their names traced back to the island.[1]

While Ireland itself was being torn by rebellion and civil war, Achill remained physically apart from direct violence. In April 1916, as the Easter Rising shook Dublin, the island could only watch events from a distance. But nearby Westport, just twenty-eight miles away, stirred with revolutionary energy. Irish Volunteers and Fianna Éireann held rallies, with nationalists like The O'Rahilly and Darrell Figgis addressing crowds on St Patrick's Day. Plans for armed action on Easter Sunday were only halted at the last moment, when Eoin MacNeill issued his countermanding order.

The Rising still left its mark. In the weeks that followed, thirty-one men from Westport were arrested and interned at Frongoch Camp in Wales, the so-called "University of Revolution." Among them was Michael Collins, who would later become Director of Intelligence for the IRA and Commander-in-Chief of the Free State Army. Collins himself wrote admiringly of Achill—not for its remoteness, but for what it symbolised in the struggle for a free Ireland:

> "In the island of Achill, impoverished as the people are... the outward aspect is a pageant... One may see processions of young women riding down on the island ponies... gathering in the turf, dressed in their shawls and in their brilliantly coloured skirts... The cottages also are little changed... It is only in such places that one gets a glimpse of what Ireland may become again... an outward sign of a prosperous and happy Gaelic life."[2]

This book does not seek to untangle the politics of the Irish Free State, but Collins's idealised view of Achill mattered—because others shared it.

In July 1923, as the Civil War gave way to uneasy peace, Chester A. Arthur III—grandson of the former U.S. President—visited the island with his wife, Charlotte. They stayed in Pollagh with Darrell and Millie Figgis, writers and cultural figures linked to the nationalist cause. Though

Ireland was scarred by conflict, Arthur saw beauty unspoiled by politics:

> "There is not a tree within miles," he wrote to his mother, "yet the huge cliffs, golden beach, purple heather hills and turquoise green sea make this one of the most beautiful places I have ever seen."[3]

Outsiders—whether Collins the revolutionary or Arthur the traveller—were struck not only by the landscape but also by the people—their honesty, resilience, and way of life. Such descriptions of Achill reinforce my understanding of those who came from the island and are vital in forming a picture of how they faced the many tragedies they endured.

In my research, I uncovered another tragedy from 1925 —one that would drive that understanding home.

By 1925, Mary's surviving siblings—Ann, Kate, and John—were all settled in Scotland. John and his wife, Lizzie, lived in Ayr. He and his eldest son, Henry, worked as Marine Firemen, shovelling coal in the boiler rooms of coastal steamships. It was gruelling work: heat, sweat, and coal dust—the most dangerous job on board.

In February of that year, the SS *Castlereagh*—also known as the *Forth Fisher*—was docked in Ayr. A cargo steamer out of Belfast, crewed mostly by men from Northern Ireland, she was loaded with coal and general goods bound for Shoreham. On 20 February, she sailed into rough seas. She never returned. By 25 February, the ship was declared lost with all hands.[4]

At first, reports listed a man named W. J. Irwin of Ship

Street, Belfast, as the ship's Marine Fireman. But when journalists knocked on his door, Irwin himself answered.

Irwin had stepped ashore. Henry took his place.

It was Henry who boarded.

It was Henry who was lost.

This cruel twist—so sudden, so steeped in irony—must have shattered John Gaughan and Henry's widow, Isabella. His mother, Lizzie, no doubt mourned his loss, but records suggest she had been estranged from John since around 1900 and had borne other children to other men. Sadly, John Gaughan died in 1947, alone; the informant on his death record was described simply as a friend.

The Steam Ship Castlereagh (The Forth Fisher).

10

THE MISSING JOURNEYMAN

My great-grandfather John Gorman hardly features in this story. While his children grew up on the streets of the Garngad, he remained conspicuously absent from the family circle. The husband, father, and journeyman shoemaker had all but slipped away.

The records preserve his life only in fragments. By 1899, his presence was already fading. That January, Barlinnie Prison recorded him convicted of "malicious mischief"—a charge that suggests desperation more than violence.[1] Likely a petty offence born of drink or frustration, it marked a turning point. The man who had once earned his keep with leather and nails was drifting into shadow.

Trouble, however, was nothing new. The earliest trace comes from a newspaper report of his involvement in a Paisley fracas in December 1877. A clipping of the report is included at the end of this chapter.[2]

In the 1901 Census the family was still together, recorded at 162 Millburn Street with John present in the household.[3]

But by November 1903 Mary—then at 236 Garngadhill—was applying for poor relief to support a medical issue with Annie. Her statement to the parish committee was blunt: she had been "deserted." John, she said, had been "idle for three months," his last known work with "Milligan, Villiers Street"—probably James Milligan & Co., the cloth merchants.[4]

Shoemaking, once a respected craft, was collapsing under the advance of mechanisation. As the trade declined, so too did John's will to keep pace.

A small clue to his movements appears the following year in Henry's 1904 army enlistment papers, which list his father as living at 4 Cobden Street. This suggests that the family had either moved again, or that there was no room for him in Mary's home—or perhaps she had forced him out and he was lodging nearby. In any case, it marked the beginning of a slow disappearance.

By the 1911 Census, John was no longer at home but recorded as an inmate of the Govan Poorhouse on Renfrew Road. It was the first trace of a long connection with Govan, halfway between Glasgow and Paisley.

In 1916, he surfaced again in a Paisley Poor Relief Committee record, giving his address as "Fairfield Street, Police Station" and describing himself as single, with no children. Earlier lodgings included the "Napier Model" at 3 Napier Street, Govan, before which he was noted as "unsettled all over the country." A typed note dated 29 August 1916 stated that he had been examined at Govan Poorhouse, but, as he was a former resident of Paisley, his case was referred to their committee.

The Paisley report, in my view, makes it clear that he had abandoned his family. Sadly, the records offer no explanation as to why.

THE MISSING JOURNEYMAN 67

These model lodging houses were grim, regimented shelters for the destitute. By 1894, Govan had three—Napier Street, Helen Street, and Craigiehall Street. A 1896 Corporation report described their residents with disdain:

> "They are of all nationalities ... disrobed clergymen and street bullies, decayed gentlemen and area sneaks, tramps, tinkers, labourers, sweeps, thieves and thimble-riggers... The moral tone is low, the habits are generally unclean, and so sometimes is the language."[5]

For John, this was not a passing refuge—it became his final address.

His sister, Sarah Ann Gorman—by then Mrs. Lafferty of 54 Storie Street, Paisley—appears in the record, though the tone suggests John was more acquaintance than brother. His older brother, Henry, is harder to trace after 1881. Official records list him as a "wool dyer," and in 1886 their mother, Sarah, stated that he was serving as a "soldier in the Ayrshire Militia." Yet multiple newspaper reports describe a Henry Gorman, dyer of Paisley, appearing repeatedly before the magistrates for petty offences linked to drink. Furthermore, a Henry Gorman died in Paisley in 1897, and I believe this was indeed John's brother. Their other sister, Maggie, died in 1905. By then, whatever family ties John may once have leaned on had loosened—or snapped.

The roots of his decline may lie in grief. His mother, Sarah, died in 1888. She had been the family's anchor after the early death of his father, Henry, in 1861. Sarah, a northern Irish woman from Keady in Armagh, had held the family together through years of moves between Paisley's poorer lanes. Perhaps something in John gave way when she was gone.

His downfall could also be attributed to a wider tide. The economy of craftsmen was dying. Trades such as shoe-making and dyeing, which had sustained working families for generations, were being overtaken by machines. Men like John found themselves stripped of their skills and left with only instability. For many, the path led to drink, prison, or the poorhouse. John's story was not unique—but for his children, it meant growing up with a father who had become a ghost.

The 1921 Census recorded Mary as a "widow." Whether this reflected legal fact under the seven-year rule, convenient fiction, or simply her acceptance that John was not coming back remains uncertain.

In reality, he appears on the same census not far away— listed again as a lodger at the Napier Lodging House, 35 Main Street, Govan. He was described as an unemployed jobbing shoemaker. Despite the short distance between Govan and the Garngad, life for Mary and the children had already moved on without him.

By then, Mary had moved back to Rosemount Street, settling at number 19—perhaps a slight improvement on 236 Garngadhill, though still cramped. The flat had only two rooms, shared by five people. For someone raised in a thatched cottage in Dooagh, where livestock often shared the hearth, such quarters may not have seemed unusual at all.

John Gorman died in 1929 at the Southern General Hospital in Govan. His last address was once again Napier House—the lodging house that had long since replaced any notion of home. The cause of death was recorded as a cerebral haemorrhage.[6]

There were no reunions, no reconciliations—only his eldest son Henry, to register the death. It was perhaps the final thread between John and the family he had left behind.

Sadly, he had missed it all: his sons marching to war, Annie's marriage, Isabella's wedding, the homecomings, the funerals, and all the quiet, everyday struggles and triumphs that shape a family. Mary carried it all—alone.

And yet, in the margins of the archive, John's story lingers. Not merely as one of abandonment, but as a reflection of a man undone by forces larger than himself. He was the missing journeyman—lost not only to his family, but to an age that no longer had use for the craft he once offered.

FIGHT AND RESCUE AT CHARLESTON.

This morning, shortly after midnight, two men were engaged fighting in Rowan Street, Charleston, and a crowd of about twenty people were looking on. The two constables on the beat interrupted the pugilistic encounter, and succeeded in seizing one of the combatants. As they were taking him off to the Police Office, a bleachfield worker, named Daniel M'Gavin, from Barterholme, came forward, incited the crowd to rescue the prisoner, and swore with an oath that the man would not be taken to the office. In company with another man, named John Gorman, shoemaker, Rowan Street, he seized on the man in custody, and with the help of others in the crowd, got him out of the hands of the constables. M'Gavin and Gorman were brought before Bailie Halden at the Police Court this morning, when the former pleaded guilty and the latter convicted on the evidence of the policemen. The magistrate imposed a fine of 15s upon each, or suffer imprisonment for 20 days.

Newspaper clipping detailing John Gorman's early brushes with notoriety. Paisley Daily Express, 25 December 1877.

The Napier Model - John Gorman's final address in Govan.

II

CHILDREN OF HER FORTITUDE

By the early 1930s, life at Rosemount Street was changing. Mary Gaughan's children—Henry, Annie, John, Isabella, James, and William—were entering new phases of adulthood, each shaped by the working-class realities that had defined their upbringing.

Annie and John remained closest to their mother after the First World War. My father often recalled that Auntie Annie and Uncle John lived together for years, bound by circumstance and shared loss. Annie, widowed in 1915, relied on a pension from the Ministry of Pensions—a vital lifeline, though one tied to strict conditions. Remarriage, or even behaviour judged improper, could see it withdrawn.

John bore his own scars. A gun-shot wound to the right leg left him with pain and limited mobility, yet he kept steady work. My father believed that his uncle had lost a leg, though I have found no record to confirm this. What is certain is that he was awarded the Silver War Badge, indicating a serious wound sustained in service.

As Mary entered her late sixties, Annie likely became the *cearchall*—the central beam of the household—shouldering much of the daily responsibility. She kept the tenement rhythms alive: tea warming on the stove, meals prepared, the quiet, endless tasks that stitched family life together.

Meanwhile, the other Gormans were establishing households of their own.

On 10 June 1931, Henry married Elizabeth Johnstone Boyd at St Mary's Church in Calton. The couple moved to Abercromby Street, leaving the Garngad behind.

Isabella—known as Bella—remained in the Garngad with her husband, James Owens, until they later relocated to Moodiesburn Street in Blackhill. Their move almost certainly reflected Glasgow Corporation's slum-clearance programme, which by 1933 had designated Blackhill as one of the new estates built to rehouse families from overcrowded districts like the Garngad.[1]

James, the second youngest, married Mary Currie on 31 December 1932 at St Roch's Church. They stayed for several years at 12 Rosemount Street before moving to Berryburn Road in Barmulloch, another of the Corporation's interwar housing schemes.

These moves mirrored a wider pattern. In the interwar years, Glasgow's housing policy shifted towards planned dispersal. Communities that had been close-knit for generations were scattered to new estates. The Garngad, once densely populated and interwoven with Irish-Scottish families, was gradually hollowing out. By 1933, it was among the first districts targeted for major slum clearance, and in 1942 its identity was reshaped again when the area was officially renamed Royston.[2]

As the Gormans built new lives, the city around them was sinking deeper into crisis. The global financial crash of 1929 struck Glasgow hard. Mary's family could not escape these realities; work was uncertain, and the city around them was hardening.

By 1931, nearly a quarter of Glasgow's workforce was unemployed. The shipyards that had once powered the Clyde had slowed to a crawl. Soup kitchens opened in places like Gallowgate and Springburn. In the Garngad, youth gangs—formed around sectarian or territorial loyalties—fought less for ideology than for belonging. The tenement streets, once alive with music, neighbourly chatter, and open doors, now echoed with sirens and police whistles.

For anyone tracing a family in Glasgow between census years, the Valuation Rolls—kept since 1855—are an invaluable resource. They became pivotal in my search for Mary after 1921, a way of keeping track of her movements. Yet after 1935, her name vanished from the rolls at 19 Rosemount Street. After more than forty years in the Garngad, she was no longer listed as a tenant. It raised a pressing question: had she died, or simply moved on? A search of Glasgow's death records yielded nothing.

For a woman who had endured life in Glasgow for four decades, it was hard for me to accept that she had simply vanished from all the records. I searched emigration lists and followed a few false leads. I checked every death entry under both Gorman and Gaughan, and even examined the lair records at Dalbeth Cemetery, where my grandparents, William and Mary Ann Gorman, were buried. But I had reached a dead end.

So I asked my father what he remembered about his grandmother. He was seventy-nine, had suffered a serious stroke the year before, and was not as sharp as he once was, but his answer was brief and certain: "She went back to Ireland. She died there. Annie took her home."

It wasn't much, but it was something to follow. Of

course, he had never met her—and I don't think any of his brothers or sisters had either—but that small story must have been passed down, in some quiet way, by his father

To find her again, I would have to return to the Irish records.

The Garngad.

12

THE LONG WAY HOME

"We return to the places we belong, even if only at the end."

In her final years, Mary watched her children grow into good, honest adults—each forging new lives and relationships of their own. Despite the hardship and sectarian unrest of the Garngad, none had ever brought trouble to her door. And as the slow dismantling of the community she had long belonged to was underway, Mary made a quiet but decisive choice.

Glasgow Corporation was moving forward with plans to clear the Garngad and rehouse families in distant estates on the city's edge.[1] I suspect that Mary, now in her seventies, had little desire to end her days in an unfamiliar scheme, far from the streets she knew by heart. At seventy-one, after a lifetime spent in cramped flats, she seems to have refused to finish her days in yet another Glasgow tenement. Instead, she must have made the decision to return to Achill—to Dooagh, where her story had first begun.

That decision was confirmed when I finally uncovered Mary's death record in the Irish records. The search, however, was not straightforward. I did not know the registration district for Achill, nor the exact year of her death, so I sifted through many entries for Mary Gorman before finally finding hers—and even then, it was not the end of the story.

In reflection, she had first crossed the Irish Sea as a teenager, joining the annual tide of tattie-hokers bound for Scotland. She had been left to raise children alone, endured bitter winters, and watched three sons return from war. Through hunger, grief, and the slow thinning of her Glasgow street, she had persevered. Her death record noted that she had been ill for some time—perhaps it was this decline that finally turned her thoughts homeward.

It was Annie who brought her there. Her name appeared on the death record as the person present at Mary's passing, confirming that I had found the right entry. I wasn't surprised. Annie had remained at her mother's side through it all. Now she would guide her back to the place of her birth. They left Rosemount Street together—two women bound by blood and, no doubt, by the quiet understanding that the end was near.

The journey itself would have been long—not only in distance, but in recollection. I have travelled the road myself, and even by modern standards it feels long; but imagine how it must have been in the mid-1930s. Transport had changed dramatically since Mary first made that journey from Dooagh—across the bogs to Achill Sound, then from Westport Quay to the west of Scotland.

By 1935, a return journey would likely have begun with a ferry from Glasgow—still Scotland's busiest port of departure. In fact, between 1900 and 1950, it ranked fourth among all ports in Britain and Ireland.[2] The route to Belfast or Dublin was well-worn by generations of migrant families.

Once in Ireland, they likely travelled by rail and road, passing through towns Mary hadn't seen in over half a century. Perhaps they followed the Great Northern Railway to Dublin, or took the western route through Athlone into Connacht. In time, they would have reached the road to Newport, with Croagh Patrick rising ahead, a silent sentinel on the horizon. From there, the path led through Mulranny to Achill Sound, where they crossed the Michael Davitt Bridge and stepped back onto the island.

By then, Achill had altered, though its heart remained the same. The old roads first laid in the 1830s by workers from the Colony had been pressed into sturdier roads by the weight of tourists, and the railway—though gone—had left its ghost upon the island. Some villages had thinned, their younger voices carried abroad on the tide of emigration, yet the land itself was unchanged. Slievemore still brooded against the sky, peat smoke drifted soft and sweet from cottage chimneys, and the Atlantic beat its endless rhythm against the cliffs. For Mary, it was not simply a return. I like to imagine that the island had held her memory in trust, waiting for her to come home.

Returning home to die in one's place of birth was nothing unusual. It was woven into the instincts of Irish and Scottish emigrants alike—a quiet pull that endured, no matter how far life had carried them. For many who had left in search of work or survival, the longing to return to the "old country" never faded. It was not just about a piece of land or a house left behind, but about belonging—about ending one's days beneath the same mountain, by the same shore, within the same parish where life had first begun.

For Mary, that meaning was simple. She would rest at home, beneath Slievemore's shadow, where the story of her life had started.

View from Dooagh, circa 1930, with Slievemore visible in the distance.

13

THE PASSING

From the death certificate I learned only the barest fact: that Mary had endured, for more than a year, a chronic intestinal obstruction. The language was clinical, stripped of emotion—just ink on paper. It gave no glimpse of how the pain came and went, how the nights stretched thin, how breath grew heavier by the hour. It could not tell who sat beside her bed, or how her fingers may have reached, even in weakness, for the comfort of a familiar hand.

Annie present at the death, and so I picture her—my great-aunt—keeping vigil at her mother's side. I see her in the stillness of a winter room, fire low in the hearth, watching Mary's face for signs of pain, for signs of peace. Annie, who had crossed the sea with her, now bore the weight Mary had once carried alone in the smoke-blackened tenements of Glasgow. The circle had closed—not in silence, and not in solitude, but in the presence of the daughter who had carried her home.

From what I have learned about the community on Achill, no one passed alone. Illness and death belonged to the community as much as to the family. When the end drew near, word would have travelled quickly through the village. Neighbours crossed thresholds without waiting to be asked, offering not just food but presence—steady, unflinching, and deeply understood. This was not charity; it was custom. It was kinship.

I can only imagine how it must have been. Some would have come to help, others simply to be near—old acquaintances, cousins twice removed, a neighbour from childhood now grey and bent with age. People might have arrived in twos and threes, coats dusted with sea mist, to take their quiet place by the bedside. They would have brought flasks of tea, pots of soup, loaves of soda bread wrapped in cloth. They would have brought prayer.

I can almost hear it: the low murmur of the Rosary circling the room, beads slipping rhythmically through calloused fingers—

"Holy Mary, Mother of God, pray for us sinners now and at the hour of our death."

The words rising and falling like the Atlantic outside the door, ancient and unchanging. Gaelic voices weaving together in devotion, a litany shaped by centuries, echoing through the house from morning until night. These prayers were not for salvation alone—they were an act of love, an anchor against fear, a way of holding her until she let go.

In my mind, the bedroom would have changed in those final days, slowly becoming a sacred space. Furniture might have been shifted to make room for chairs, a lamp kept low, the window perhaps cracked open to let the soul pass. Children may have been kept just beyond the doorway, hushed but watchful, absorbing the weight of what was happening. Someone might have lit candles. Someone might have washed her hands.

And when her passing came—if it was as I imagine—it would not have been into silence, but into that steady chorus of breath and prayer. She would have left not as a patient, but as a matriarch, borne to the edge of death by the same hands that had fed and clothed and comforted her in life.

On 21 January 1936, Mary Gaughan passed away in Dooagh, beneath Slievemore's quiet slopes, aged seventy-one—her long journey ending where it had begun.

14

SINGING THE SOUL HOME

"May the road rise up to meet you, may the wind be always at your back, may the sun shine warm upon your face; the rains fall soft upon your fields, and until we meet again, may God hold you in the palm of his hand." — The Irish Blessing of St Patrick.

After Mary's passing, her wake would almost certainly have begun at once. A Gaelic wake was not merely custom but ritual, carried from generation to generation. Each stage held meaning: the keening—like singing the soul home—would have risen like wind through the rafters, giving voice to grief too sharp for words; the children brought to touch her still hands, a tender initiation into the mystery of mortality; the chairs overturned, the threshold swept—signs to guard the soul on its journey.

Mary Gaughan's wake in Dooagh in 1936 would likely have followed these deep-rooted Irish traditions of mourning—where sorrow and celebration met. The wake was both farewell and gathering: a time of tears, prayer, and laughter shared around the hearth. Neighbours and kin might have crowded into the house, some bringing food, others simply bringing their presence. For a woman who had known hardship and come home to die among her own, the wake was not only a goodbye—it was, I imagine, a tribute to a life marked by strength, sorrow, and love.

The mood would have reflected her age and long illness: mournful, yes, but not tragic. There is a particular tenderness reserved for those who return home to die—a kind of peace folded into grief. Songs may have been sung beside the fire, memories passed hand to hand like cups of tea—or stronger drink. In the dark of winter, such warmth mattered.

Among the older women, stories of Mary's youth were likely shared: the family she came from in Dooagh, her journey to Scotland as a young girl, the hard years in Glasgow. Her life, stretched between two worlds, became a thread for others to follow—a way of making sense of their own journeys. These conversations, hushed and vivid, were part of the wake's purpose too: to remember, to teach, to bind the living to the dead.

Mary's wake belonged to an older tradition. The Irish wake stretches back through centuries, its origins lost to time but shaped by both Christian ritual and echoes of older Celtic belief. Death was never the end, but a passage. The body was never left alone. Candles burned through the night, and loved ones kept vigil in turns. Mirrors were covered, clocks stopped—tokens of care for the soul on its journey. Beneath the folklore, a deeper truth endured: the wake was a space of kinship, presence, and memory.

Food and drink circulated, not to dull sorrow but to share it—reminding all present that life carried on even as one thread was cut. Then came the final journey. The road to the grave carried Mary four miles up the mountain, each step both physical and symbolic, returning her to the land that had shaped her.

The grave itself was not left to hired men but, as was the custom, dug by neighbours—spades striking into soil heavy with memory. When the coffin was lifted, it rested not on the shoulders of strangers but on those of kin and community: each step a vow of remembrance, each pause a mark of love.

No written record tells us who stood in the cold air of Slievemore that winter, but based on family ties I can picture them—my great-uncles Henry, John, and James; my great-aunt Bella; her kin Frank and Kate McNamara among the mourners; and the wider circle of O'Donnells, Pattens, and Gallaghers—families whose lives had been braided with hers through land, labour, and marriage. Together they carried her, not just to the grave, but into the enduring memory of the island itself.

The image my father recalled—that of a woman kneeling at a grave beneath a mountain—was true. That mountain was Slievemore, the ancient burial ground of the Gaughans and of many Achill families. When I journeyed there in search of Mary's story, John McNamara kindly took me to the site. But as soon as we set foot in that old cemetery, the heavens opened, and we had to abandon our search for Mary's grave—and the other Gaughans'. I returned later that day, and in the quiet of reflection, my father's memory stirred into life. Among the leaning stones, with the Atlantic wind in my face and the mountain looming above, I could almost see her. In that moment, my father's vision and my own converged, and the truth of her return was no longer imagined, but deeply felt.

I could find no trace of Mary's grave, but I know she lies there still—at peace—while the wild winds and the murmur of the Atlantic keep an everlasting requiem over her.

Her story was not only one of return, but of connection —of carrying a place within her. She brought Achill into Glasgow's streets, and she carried Glasgow back into Achill. She belonged to both: a daughter of the island, a mother of the Garngad, and a thread stretched forever between two shores.

Slievemore Old Cemetery looking towards the Minuan Heights.

THE CEARCHALL

After laying Mary to rest, Annie Gorman returned to Rosemount Street—a street that had carried her family through decades of hope and hardship. She and John lived together, neither of them marrying. I can only imagine that they found a quiet companionship, bound by the lingering impact the First World War had left on their lives.

As Glasgow changed, so did their surroundings. The old soot-darkened tenements gave way to demolition, and Annie and John were rehoused on Frankfield Street, in the Blackhilll where the other Gormans hand ended up. There, life found its rhythm again: tea steaming in chipped mugs, a window left open to catch the murmur of the street outside. In small ways, they would have kept Mary's spirit alive—the cearchall holding firm even as the past slipped quietly into history.

But the Gaughan and Gorman story did not end in stillness. William, Mary's youngest, carried the family name forward. He also moved to Blackhill, Queenslie Street. A labourer, soldier, steelworker, and father of eleven, he raised four daughters and seven sons through years of economic strain and world conflict. When another war came, the Gormans answered the call. Three of the sons served in the war or towards the end of it and Auntie Isa (Isabella) joined the Women's Land Army, and even William, in his mid-forties, enlisted.

Strangely, the Second World War took its toll in a different way. The only life lost was that of another of Mary's sons-in-law—poor James Owens, who had suffered during the First World War. He died in August 1944 of a heart attack while serving as a night watchman with the Civil Defence Force. Once again, all the other Gormans who had served returned home safely.

In time, the generation shaped under Mary's care began to fade. Annie, steadfast and devoted, died in 1957. Henry, the eldest son and long-serving soldier, died the same year. James, the chemical worker and veteran, passed in 1960. Isabella and John followed in 1962, closing a chapter that had begun in Glasgow's industrial heart. William, the bridge to the next generation, died on 19 November 1968.

In the years that followed, the Gorman name scattered across Glasgow—Royston, Blackhill, and Barmulloch. The world around them changed beyond recognition: the factories that once thundered fell silent, and the tenements that had held generations of families were torn down. Yet through this story, the memory of the Gaughans and the Gormans endures—carried forward in words, in remembrance, and in the act of tracing their journey from Achill to Glasgow and back again.

And so Mary's story continues—through her children, her descendants, and these pages that preserve her life and legacy. From the Garngad's stone closes to the cliffs of Slievemore, her presence lingers, bridging island and city, Ireland and Scotland, past and present. Beneath the Atlantic wind and the shifting Glasgow sky, her story endures—quiet, steadfast, and unbroken.

Blackhill tenements, Queenslie Street — the home where my grandfather lived and my father was born.

BLOODLINES - THE GAUGHAN'S OF ACHILL ISLAND

In Achill's past, families were never separate lines running in parallel. They were interwoven through marriages, baptisms, and landholdings—a web of kinship that bound neighbours together for generations. Certain surnames dominate the island's story: McNamara, Kilbane, Lavelle, O'Malley, Henaghan, Patten, Gallagher, Toolis, O'Donnell —and the Gaughans are entwined with them all.

The Gaughans were regarded as "aboriginal Irish," their lineage deeply rooted in Achill's soil, in contrast to other parts of Ireland reshaped by settlers and newcomers.[1] They first step clearly into the written record in Griffith's Valuation (1847–1864), where a **Thomas Gaughan** is listed in Dooagh. Though little else is known of his life, his name on the valuation rolls signifies more than tenancy—it represents continuity, a family holding its ground on the island's rugged edge.

He was most likely the father of **Henry (Harry) Gaughan**, who in 1854 married **Mary O'Donnell of Dooagh** at St Thomas's Chapel of Ease in Dugort. That single entry marks more than a union: it connects two long-standing Achill families—the Gaughans and the O'Donnells—and ties them to the land through their fathers, Thomas and Pat, both named as tenants in the parish records.

Harry's life can be traced only in fragments. His marriage certificate names him a labourer; his death certificate (1890) records him as a farmer and fisherman. Like so many Achill men, he likely moved between labouring, farming, and fishing as seasons and tides dictated—occupations that left few written traces but sustained a family against the harsh Atlantic. He raised several children in Dooagh, and through them the Gaughans became connected to many of the island's enduring families.

Mary, of course, married into the Gorman family of County Armagh. **Thomas** married **Bridget Patten** of Bunacurry, whose daughter Ann later joined the **Fadian** family. **Catherine (Kate)** wed **John Donnelly**, and one of their daughters married into the **McNamara** line. **Ann** married **Anthony McGowan**, a Scot, extending the family's reach to Linlithgow. **John**, the youngest surviving son, married **Lizzie Crossley** of Ayrshire, whose family were long tied to the sea. The twins, **Pat and Martin**, left only faint traces—Pat likely dying in 1895, Martin vanishing from the records—and **Bridget**, the youngest, died in childhood.

Through these marriages and migrations, the Gaughans became entwined with the **O'Donnells, Pattens, Fadians, Donnellys, McNamaras, Gormans, McGowans, and Crossleys.** Their story is not one of isolation, but of deep interconnection—rooted in Achill, extended outward through marriage, labour, and memory, carried across Scotland's fields and Glasgow's closes.

On the following pages are a family tree for **Mary**

Gaughan and a direct-descendant chart leading to me. A full genealogy is beyond these pages, though to date **168 families** have been traced directly to **Henry and Mary Gaughan**—and more may yet emerge from parish registers or family recollections. Their absence here is not a conclusion but an invitation: the story of the Gaughans—like Achill itself—remains unfinished, unfolding still with every new record uncovered.

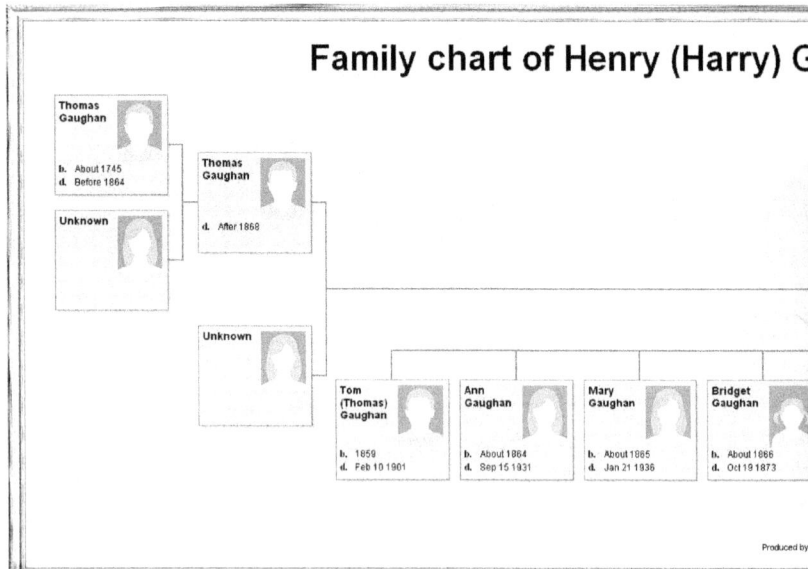

and Mary Gaughan [O'Donnell]

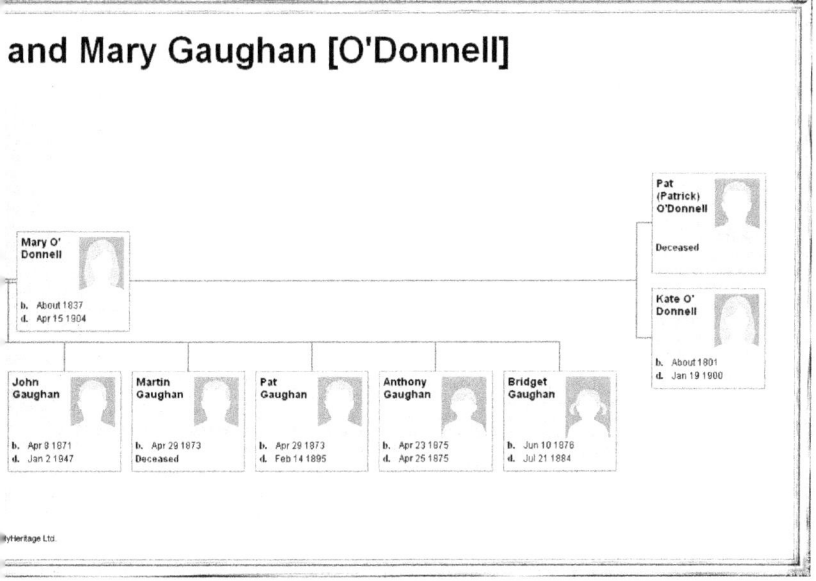

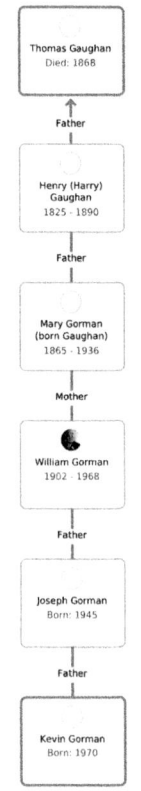

SUMMARY OF GENEALOGICAL RESOURCES USED

Tracing the life of my great-grandmother, her family, and their connections across Achill Island and Scotland required piecing together records from multiple archives and databases. No single source told the whole story—each provided fragments that, when combined, revealed the broader picture.

• **Irish Vital Records** came from *RootsIreland.ie* (subscription) and *IrishGenealogy.ie* (free), which provided births, deaths, marriages, and some parish and census substitute material. Griffith's Valuation and gravestone inscriptions were crucial for identifying early family links on Achill Island.

• **Scottish Records** were accessed through *ScotlandsPeople* (pay-per-view) for vital records, census entries, and valuation rolls, supported by Poor Law indexes from Paisley and the Glasgow Mitchell Library's extensive family history holdings.

• **Online Databases** like *Ancestry*, *Findmypast*, and *Forces War Records* helped cross-reference military service, migration, and family trees.

- **Archival Collections** from the National Archives of Ireland, the National Archives (UK), the National Library of Ireland, and *AskAboutIreland.ie* filled in historical and contextual detail, especially census returns, parish registers, and landholding patterns.

By drawing on these diverse sources—civil, parish, legal, and personal—it was possible to reconstruct a family narrative that spanned both sides of the Irish Sea.

Notes

1. OILEÁN ACLA

1. William Wilde, *Narrative of a Voyage to Madeira, Tenerife and Along the Shores of the Mediterranean* (Dublin, 1840).
2. Achill Heritage Centre, "Achill History," https://achillheritagecentre.wordpress.com/achill-history-2/, accessed 8 July 2025.

2. THE COLONY: THE PRICE OF SOUP

1. Patricia Byrne, *The Preacher and the Prelate: The Achill Mission Colony and the Battle for Souls in Famine Ireland* (Dublin: Merrion Press, 2018). See also Desmond Fennell, *The Achill Mission Colony, 1831–1861* (Dublin: Columba Press, 1968).
2. Byrne, *Preacher and the Prelate*, pp. 32–34; Fennell, *Achill Mission Colony*, pp. 47–52. Figures on the number of schools in 1835 are drawn from these accounts.
3. Irene Whelan, *The Bible War in Ireland: The "Second Reformation" and the Polarization of Protestant-Catholic Relations, 1800–1840* (Madison: University of Wisconsin Press, 2005).
4. Irene Whelan, *The Bible War in Ireland: The "Second Reformation" and the Polarization of Protestant-Catholic Relations, 1800–1840* (Madison: University of Wisconsin Press, 2005).
5. *Griffith's Primary Valuation of Tenements, County Mayo, 1855*, available via Ask About Ireland (www.askaboutireland.ie).
6. Church of Ireland Registers, Achill Parish (baptisms, marriages, burials), Representative Church Body Library, Dublin. Entries for the Gaughan and Masterton families note recantations in 1845 and subsequent years.
7. Church of Ireland, Dugort, Marriage Register, 1854. Entry for the marriage of Henry Gaughan and Mary O'Donnell, conducted by Rev. Joseph Barker and witnessed by Rev. John Vickers. Register held at the Representative Church Body Library, Dublin.
8. Marriage (Ireland) Act 1844 (7 & 8 Vict. c. 81); Civil Registration Act (Ireland) 1845; General Register Office of Ireland, *Guide to Civil Registration Records*.
9. Weekly Register and Catholic Standard, 03 October 1863, p.211.

3. DOOAGH: A VILLAGE ON THE EDGE

1. T. McDonald, *Achill Island – Archaeology – History – Folklore* (Tullamore: IAS Publications, 2006), p. 343.
2. *Illustrated London News*, 23 March 1844, p. 8.
3. *Freeman's Journal*, 22 October 1895, p.6.
4. *Farmer's Gazette and Journal of Practical Horticulture*, 28 December 1878, p. 9.
5. John Harris, *Ireland Today and Tomorrow* (London: T. Fisher Unwin, 1906), quoted in *Achill History*, Achill Heritage Centre, https://achillheritagecentre.wordpress.com/achill-history-2/ (accessed 10 August 2025).
6. Patrick Joseph Joyce, "Biggest village in Europe," *Irish Independent*, [exact date] 1920, p. 4.
7. *Mayo Constitution*, 24 January 1860, p. 3.
8. *Petty Sessions Court Registers, Achill*, 15 January 1861 (National Archives of Ireland).
9. *Petty Sessions Court Registers, Westport*, 1905 (National Archives of Ireland).

4. THE ROAD TO PAISLEY

1. Patrick Joseph Joyce, *A Forgotten Part of Ireland*, 1910, pp. 160–161.
2. Paisley Poor Law Records, Application/Relief Registers, Series 12, Statement No. 29135, Paisley Heritage Centre (Renfrewshire Council). Unless otherwise stated, all Poor Law references for Mary Gaughan and family are drawn from this collection.

5. THE MACHINERY OF MIGRATION

1. Dictionary of the Scots Language, s.v. "howk," https://dsl.ac.uk.
2. Tom Gillespie, *"Achill's tattie hokers worked in 'slavish conditions,'"* Connaught Telegraph, 15 Oct 2022.
3. Testimony attributed to Mary O'Donnell of Achill, aged eighteen, was printed in the Falkirk Herald on 21 November 1900.
4. **Hansard**, *Ayrshire Potato Diggers*, vol. 192, debated on Thursday, 9 July 1908, House of Commons. Available at: https://hansard.parliament.uk/commons/1908-07-09/debates/ba29b071-83c9-4b49-a2de-28a5b26dbdc3/AyrshirePotatoDiggers
5. Evening Herald (Dublin), 13 July 1918, p. 1
6. *The Scotsman*. 19 Nov. 1938, p. 14.

7. Anne O'Dowd, *Spalpeens and Tattie Hokers: History and Folklore of the Irish Migratory Agricultural Worker in Ireland and Britain* (Dublin: Irish Academic Press, 1991), esp. p. 199, as discussed in "Na Spailpíní: Irish Seasonal Labourers in Britain in the 20th Century," *The Dustbin of History* blog (2013); see also RTÉ Archives, "Irish Potato Pickers in Scotland," and RTÉ Documentary on One, "The Tattie Hokers," with recordings from O'Dowd's fieldwork.

6. SHADOWS OVER ACHILL

1. Civil Registration of Deaths, Ireland, Westport District, entry for Henry Gaughan, 1890 (occupation listed as "Farmer & Fisherman").
2. Paisley Poor Law Records, Application/Relief Registers, Series 1q, Statement No. 22295, Paisley Heritage Centre (Renfrewshire Council), application of Bridget Gaughan, 25 Maxwellton Street, 1893.
3. *Freeman's Journal*, 19 February 1894, p. 6; *Connaught Telegraph*, 18 August 1894, p. 3 – reports on extensions of the Westport–Achill railway.
4. *Mayo News*, 16 June 1894; *Western People*, 16 June 1894; *Connaught Telegraph*, 20 June 1894 – reports on the Cloughmore "Clew Bay Disaster."
5. McDonald, T., *Achill Island – Archaeology – History – Folklore* (IAS Publications, Tullamore, 2006), pp. 229 – prophecy of Red Brian Carabine.
6. *Mayo News*, 23 June 1894, – funeral account of the victims at Kildavnet Cemetery.
7. Paisley Poor Law Records, Application/Relief Registers, Series 11, Statement No. 33560, Paisley Heritage Centre (Renfrewshire Council), application of James Gaughan.

9. BEYOND THE HORIZON

1. Commonwealth War Graves Commission. "Sheridan, Richard Brinsley." *CWGC Database of War Dead, First World War*.https://www.cwgc.org, accessed August 2025.
2. Michael Collins, *A Path to Freedom*, Cork, Mercier Press, 1968 (UCC CELT online ed.), chapter *"View of Life in the Achill Gaeltacht"*.
3. Chester A. Arthur III, letter to his mother, July 1923, as quoted in *"Letter describes 'extraordinarily beautiful' Achill Island in summer 1923,"* Mark Holan's Irish American Blog, accessed August 2025 https://www.markholan.org/archives/15391

4. Dorset Heritage Explorer, "Maritime Record MWX2206 – Castlereagh (Firth Fisher)", Heritage Dorset, record MWX2206

10. THE MISSING JOURNEYMAN

1. Scottish Prison Registers, Barlinnie Prison, January 1899, National Records of Scotland.
2. *Paisley Daily Express*, 25 December 1877, p. 2.
3. Scotland Census, 1901, 162 Millburn Street, Glasgow. Unless otherwise stated, all census references are drawn from Scotland Census records (National Records of Scotland).
4. Glasgow Poor Law Records, Series 7, Statement 1774, Glasgow Mitchell Library. Unless otherwise stated, all Poor Law references for Mary Gorman and family are drawn from this collection.
5. Glasgow Corporation, *Report of the Medical Officer of Health for the Year 1896*, as cited in *Ross Street Lodging House* photograph caption, TheGlasgowStory.com, image TGSA00814.
6. Statutory Register of Deaths, John Gorman, 1929, Southern General Hospital, Govan, National Records of Scotland.

11. CHILDREN OF HER FORTITUDE

1. *Glasgow Corporation Housing Department, First Annual Report on Housing (Glasgow, 1933), pp. 12–14; see also T. C. Smout, A Century of the Scottish People, 1830–1950* (London: Collins, 1986), pp. 239–41.
2. *"Royston (formerly Garngad)," TheGlasgowStory, Glasgow City Archives, Housing Department Collection, accessed [date], https://www.theglasgowstory.com.*

12. THE LONG WAY HOME

1. Glasgow Corporation Housing Department, Annual Report, 1933, Glasgow City Archives.
2. Board of Trade, Statistical Abstract for the United Kingdom, 1930, HMSO.

BLOODLINES - THE GAUGHAN'S OF ACHILL ISLAND

1. *Leave Your Hat at the Sound,* RTÉ DocArchive, 1974. https://www.rte.ie/radio/doconone/646800-radio-documentary-leave-your-hat-at-the-sound

ACKNOWLEDGMENTS

The story of Mary Gaughan could never have been pieced together alone. In the absence of oral tradition or family memory, this book rests on the careful work of archivists, genealogists, and local historians who preserve the scattered traces of ordinary lives.

My thanks go to Brendan Walsh at the North Mayo Heritage Centre, whose research into Achill's records formed the foundation for tracing Mary's beginnings. His knowledge of the island's history and landscape gave her story its true setting.

I am indebted to the staff of the Genealogy Centre at the Mitchell Library, Glasgow. Their patient guidance through archives, census returns, and city registers opened up the world Mary entered after leaving Achill. Their dedication to making public history accessible gave this project its shape.

Thanks also to Bryan Smith at the Heritage Centre in Paisley. His help in uncovering Poor Law records and local context added depth and texture to chapters that might otherwise have remained incomplete.

But above all, I am grateful to John McNamara of Keelwest, Dooagh. His generosity went far beyond walking me through the lanes of Keelwest, showing me the home of my relations, and guiding me to Slievemore and other key sites across the island. He also read through my chapters, answered countless questions, and offered corrections and insights that only someone steeped in Achill life could provide. Without him, I might have felt like a stranger in a place meant to be home; instead, through his knowledge and kindness, I found not only clarity in the past but a genuine bond with it.

Each of these individuals gave their time, expertise, and insight with generosity. Without them, Mary Gaughan's story would be far less clear. This book is stronger, truer, and more deeply rooted because of their contributions.

And though the story within these pages has come to a close, my own bond with Achill is only beginning—late in life, perhaps, but no less real. What began as a search for the past has become a return of its own: a thread tying me, at last, to the island that shaped my family and still whispers beneath Slievemore and in the memory of its people.

BIBLIOGRAPHY

Primary Sources

Achill Missionary Herald and Western Witness. Achill, Ireland: Mission Press, 1837–1869.

Arthur, Chester A. III. Letter to his mother, July 1923. Quoted in Mark Holan, "An American President's Grandson Visits Achill, 1923." *Mark Holan's Irish-American Blog*, 2023. https://www.markholan.org/archives/15391.

Board of Trade. *Statistical Abstract for the United Kingdom*. London: HMSO, 1930.

Collins, Michael. *The Path to Freedom*. Dublin: Talbot Press, 1922.

Department of Agriculture and Technical Instruction for Ireland. *Report of the Departmental Committee on Migratory Labourers from Ireland to Scotland* (Cd. 2828). Parliamentary Papers, 1900. Appendix: Evidence of Mary O'Donnell (Achill).

Evening Herald (Dublin), July 13, 1918, 1.

Farmer's Gazette and Journal of Practical Horticulture, December 28, 1878, 9.

Freeman's Journal, October 1895, 6.

Griffith, Richard. *Griffith's Valuation, 1847–1864*. OMS Services Ltd., Eneclann Ltd., and the National Library of Ireland, 2003. Accessed July 2025. http://www.askaboutireland.ie/griffith-valuation/index.xml.

Hansard Parliamentary Debates. "Ayrshire Potato Diggers." Vol. 192. House of Commons, 9 July 1908. https://hansard.parliament.uk/commons/1908-07-09/debates/ba29b071-83c9-4b49-a2de-28a5b26dbdc3/AyrshirePotatoDiggers.

Illustrated London News, March 23, 1844, 8.

Irish Independent, 1920, 4.

Joyce, Patrick Joseph. *A Forgotten Part of Ireland*. Tuam: Self-published, 1910.

Mayo Constitution, January 24, 1860, 3.

Mayo News, June 1894 (reporting the Clew Bay Disaster).

North Mayo Family History Centre. *Research on the Family of Henry Gaughan & Mary O'Donnell of Slievemore (Dooagh), Achill, Co. Mayo*. Research report, May 2025.

Paisley Daily Express, December 25, 1877, 2.

Paisley Poor Law Records. *Application/Relief Registers,* Series 12, Statement No. 29135. Paisley Heritage Centre (Renfrewshire Council).

Petty Sessions Court Registers, Achill, January 15, 1861. National Archives of Ireland.

Petty Sessions Court Registers, Westport, 1905. National Archives of Ireland.

Weekly Register and Catholic Standard, October 3, 1863, 211.

Secondary Sources

George, Tony. *Clyde Built: A History of Shipbuilding on the River Clyde.* Glasgow: William Collins, 1990.

Ghiobúin, Mealla Ní. *Dugort, Achill Island 1831–1861: The Rise and Fall of a Missionary Community.* Dublin and Portland, OR: Irish Academic Press, 2001.

Gillespie, Tom. "Achill's tattie hokers worked in 'slavish conditions.'" *Connaught Telegraph,* October 15, 2022.

Levitt, Ian S. *Poverty and Welfare in Scotland, 1890–1948.* Edinburgh: Edinburgh University Press, 1988.

McDonald, T. *Achill Island: Archaeology – History – Folklore.* Tullamore, Co. Offaly: IAS Publications, 2006.

McDonnell, Hugh. *The Clyde: River and Firth.* London: Batsford, 1963.

Mitchell, Iain R. *Orange, Green and Red: Class, Community and Conflict on Clydeside.* Glasgow: Clydebank Press, 1992.

O'Hara, Bernard, ed. *Mayo: Aspects of Its Heritage.* Galway: Archaeological, Historical and Folklore Society, Regional Technical College, 1982.

Pacione, Michael. *Housing, Segregation and Change in the Inner City: A Case Study of Glasgow.* London: Routledge, 1980.

The Glasgow Story. "Model Lodging Houses." Accessed September 2025. https://www.theglasgowstory.com/image/?inum=TGSA00814.

ABOUT THE AUTHOR

Kevin Gorman was born in the East End of Glasgow and has family roots on Achill Island, Ireland. His great-grandmother, Mary Gaughan, emigrated to Glasgow in the late 19th century, where she raised her family within the city's Irish community.

Her story inspired *The Cearchall*, a historical biography tracing her life from Achill to Scotland against the backdrop of migration, faith, and working-class life.

Kevin's research draws on archival sources and local history to explore how ordinary people endured and adapted through poverty, migration, and social change. During his History degree at Birkbeck, University of London, he focused on Irish history from the Great Famine through to the War of Independence—studies that helped shape the foundations of this work.

He holds a Master's degree from Brunel University and works in cybersecurity in the City of London. A member of the Glasgow & West of Scotland Family History Society and the Genealogical Society of Ireland, Kevin has a long-standing interest in history, genealogy, and self-publishing, using his work to uncover the stories often left out of official records.

Printed in Dunstable, United Kingdom